# Property & Casualty Exam Practice Questions

# Dear Future Exam Success Story

First of all, **THANK YOU** for purchasing Mometrix study materials!

Second, congratulations! You are one of the few determined test-takers who are committed to doing whatever it takes to excel on your exam. **You have come to the right place.** We developed these practice tests with one goal in mind: to deliver you the best possible approximation of the questions you will see on test day.

Standardized testing is one of the biggest obstacles on your road to success, which only increases the importance of doing well in the high-pressure, high-stakes environment of test day. Your results on this test could have a significant impact on your future, and these practice tests will give you the repetitions you need to build your familiarity and confidence with the test content and format to help you achieve your full potential on test day.

**Your success is our success**

**We would love to hear from you!** If you would like to share the story of your exam success or if you have any questions or comments in regard to our products, please contact us at **800-673-8175** or **support@mometrix.com**.

Thanks again for your business and we wish you continued success!

Sincerely,
The Mometrix Test Preparation Team

Copyright © 2020 by Mometrix Media LLC. All rights reserved.
Written and edited by the Mometrix Exam Secrets Test Prep Team
Printed in the United States of America

# TABLE OF CONTENTS

| | |
|---|---|
| PRACTICE TEST #1 | 1 |
| ANSWER KEY AND EXPLANATIONS | 22 |
| PRACTICE TEST #2 | 33 |
| ANSWER KEY AND EXPLANATIONS | 53 |
| THANK YOU | 64 |

# Practice Test #1

**1. A surety bond is a contract between three parties. Which of the three parties guarantees the contract will be fulfilled in its entirety?**

　　a. The guarantee
　　b. The guarantor
　　c. The reinsurance carrier
　　d. The guarantee and guarantor

**2. A surety bond is a type of insurance contract that involves at least three parties. Which party is responsible for actually performing the work being insured?**

　　a. The principal
　　b. The guarantor
　　c. The obligee
　　d. The obligee and principal

**3. What makes a fidelity bond different from a regular bond?**

　　a. Fidelity bonds can be traded.
　　b. Fidelity bonds can accrue interest.
　　c. Fidelity bonds cannot be traded.
　　d. Regular bonds cannot be traded.

**4. Trevor recently purchased his first home. Trevor is searching for an insurance policy to protect his home, which is valued at $250,000. One carrier is requiring Trevor to purchase limits of at least 80% of what his home is worth. What requirement does this insurance carrier have which requires 80% of the value to be insured?**

　　a. Coinsurance clause
　　b. Co-pay clause
　　c. Deductible clause
　　d. Valued added clause

**5. In order for a person to purchase an insurance policy, what is the potential insured required to have in relation to the exposure being insured?**

　　a. Signed proof of ownership
　　b. Full premium payment up front
　　c. Proof of funds to pay future premium payments
　　d. An insurable interest in the exposure

**6. Insurance carriers use different means of collecting data in order to determine the rates for their products. What is one concept insurance carriers use that believes that as the sample size in question grows, the average of results obtained from this sample will be closer to the expected value?**

　　a. Probability theory
　　b. Law of large numbers
　　c. Insurance rate probability
　　d. Law of probability

7. Scott purchased stocks as a means of investing his money in hopes of a great return. What type of risk is Scott taking by purchasing stocks?

   a. Pure risk
   b. Stable risk
   c. Assumed risk
   d. Speculative risk

8. Simon purchased a car with his savings from the past three years. What type of risk is Simon taking by purchasing his new car?

   a. Pure risk
   b. Stable risk
   c. Assumed risk
   d. Speculative risk

9. Builder's risk insurance is often a requirement of which party the contractor has a contract with?

   a. The future homeowner
   b. The owner of the land
   c. Local city government
   d. Builder's risk insurance is never a requirement but rather just something preferred by builders.

10. Builder's risk insurance policies typically exclude all the following exposures EXCEPT

   a. flood.
   b. wind in coastal areas.
   c. theft.
   d. earthquake.

11. Martin was the owner of a large media corporation that operated out of a single building downtown. Martin's building was badly damaged from a hurricane and had to close for several weeks for repair. Which of the following was an indirect loss of the hurricane?

   a. The building damage
   b. Lost wages from employees not being able to work
   c. The sidewalk requiring repair outside of Martin's building
   d. The roof leaking from strong winds

12. Kendall's house was located right on the beach in a popular shore town. Kendall's town sustained significant wind damage and flooding following a tropical storm. Which of the following is a direct loss Kendall suffered from the tropical storm?

   a. Hotel costs while her house is repaired
   b. Damage to her roof requiring repair
   c. Inconvenience of having a longer commute to work due to living in a hotel
   d. Increased cost of food due to having to eat at restaurants instead of being able to cook at home

**13. All of the following are types of hazards which cause concern for insurance companies as they assume different risks EXCEPT**

   a. age hazard.
   b. moral hazard.
   c. morale hazard.
   d. physical hazard.

**14. Peter was cleaning up his yard after a heavy storm hit his area the previous night. The storm brought damage such as broken tree limbs, branches, and leaves scattered across Peter's yard. Peter raked up all the debris but left it on his sidewalk without properly putting it in trash bags for removal. Peter leaving the debris on his sidewalk where the public walks through represents what type of hazard?**

   a. Moral hazard
   b. Physical debris removal hazard
   c. Morale hazard
   d. Physical hazard

**15. What type of hazard exists when the insured's attitude is poor towards the care or maintenance of the property because the insured knows insurance will cover any losses that may occur?**

   a. Moral hazard
   b. Ethical hazard
   c. Morale hazard
   d. Physical hazard

**16. Brenton needed to obtain an insurance policy in order to rent an apartment. Brenton has a terrible credit score but knew he needed to lie about his credit in order to get this apartment. He lied on his insurance application about his credit history in hopes that the company would not check his credit report. What type of hazard did Brenton participate in?**

   a. Moral hazard
   b. Ethical hazard
   c. Morale hazard
   d. Physical hazard

**17. The declarations page, or dec page, of an insurance policy contains all the following information EXCEPT**

   a. the name of the insured.
   b. policy limits.
   c. location of risk being insured.
   d. policy exclusions.

**18. Which section of the insurance policy will indicate what hazards the insured is protected against through the policy?**

   a. The declarations
   b. The insuring agreement
   c. The exclusions
   d. The hazards agreement

**19.** The insurance contract contains multiple sections to address what the policy covers, who is covered and when coverage will end. What section of the insurance contract or policy states how the policy will handle changes in coverage during the policy period?

   a. The declarations
   b. The insuring agreement
   c. Policy conditions
   d. Policy exclusions

**20.** Terrance was reading over his insurance policy to see if he had the proper coverage he felt his exposures required. Terrance read that his vehicle was covered except if he was driving the vehicle for a reason other than personal use. Which section is Terrance reading which would say this vehicle did not have coverage during specific times?

   a. The declarations
   b. The insuring agreement
   c. Policy conditions
   d. Policy exclusions

**21.** What value is determined by subtracting the depreciation from the replacement cost value of a specific piece of property?

   a. Actual cash value
   b. Depreciation cash value
   c. Wear and tear value
   d. Actual value plus

**22.** If an insured's policy calls for the insurance company to replace property with the same or equal value in the event of a loss, this is known as what type of loss valuation?

   a. Actual cash value
   b. Actual replace cost
   c. Like-new cost
   d. Replacement cost

**23.** Inventory storage, unauthorized instructions, and employee dishonesty are some examples of theft exclusions under policies containing what type of cause of loss form?

   a. Special form
   b. Standard form
   c. Broad form
   d. Policy provision form

**24.** Caroline owned a building in town that housed multiple businesses. A severe winter storm hit the town where Caroline's building was and left large amounts of snow and sleet on the roof. Part of Caroline's roof collapsed due to the weight of the snow and sleet left from this storm. Would Caroline be covered for the damaged roof by her Insurance policy if the cause of loss was broad form?

   a. No, broad form excludes any roof damage.
   b. Yes, broad form does include coverage due to the weight causing the roof to collapse.
   c. No, broad form does not include coverage when the cause of loss is weight due to snow and sleet.
   d. No, broad form excludes any weather-related losses.

25. Broad cause of loss form is available on some commercial property insurance policies. Broad cause of loss adds additional causes of loss to those already covered under basic form. All of the following are additional perils broad form will cover in addition to those covered under basic form EXCEPT
   a. falling objects.
   b. collapse.
   c. lightning.
   d. weight from snow.

26. Jason owned a home in the city that he rented out to a full-time tenant. As part of the lease for this home, Jason required his tenant to obtain an insurance policy to cover the tenant's own personal property in the home. What type of homeowner's policy should Jason's tenant obtain?
   a. HO-2
   b. HO-3
   c. HO-4
   d. HO-6

27. Which type of homeowner's policy provides coverage for the dwelling, personal property, and other structures on an all risks basis?
   a. HO-2
   b. HO-5
   c. HO-6
   d. HO-8

28. Trevor obtained an HO-2 form of homeowners insurance for his newly acquired house. What cause of loss form is attached to Trevor's HO-2 policy?
   a. Basic form
   b. Simple form
   c. All Perils form
   d. Broad form

29. The HO-3 homeowners policy is a unique policy in that it covers the dwelling and scheduled personal property on an all risks and perils basis, but what exposures does it cover on a broad-named basis?
   a. Unscheduled personal property
   b. Other structures
   c. The HO-3 does not provide coverage on a broad-named basis for any exposure.
   d. The HO-3 provides only broad-named perils coverage for all exposures, including the dwelling.

30. The HO-3 and HO-6 homeowner's forms are similar in that they provide coverage for owner occupants. These two forms however are different in that the HO-6 policy form
   a. provides more property coverage than the HO-3.
   b. provides less property coverage than the HO-3.
   c. The HO-3 and HO-6 are not similar as the HO-6 is designed for tenant coverage.
   d. The HO-6 does not provide medical payments coverage.

**31. Beth was excited to purchase her first home, which was a historic Victorian home in the city. Because of the nature of her house, Beth's insurance agent suggested she purchase an HO-8 modified homeowners policy to meet her needs. The HO-8 policy covers against exposures through what cause of loss form?**

    a. Broad form
    b. All risk
    c. Basic form
    d. Standard policy perils form

**32. Margaret owned a home in a neighborhood that had sidewalks to connect each house. All the homeowners were required to maintain the sidewalk outside of their individual homes. A significant ice storm hit and after the storm was over, Margaret left her house to drive to work without shoveling her driveway. A neighbor was walking his dog and slipped on the ice on Margaret's driveway causing him to break his arm. Margaret is guilty of what when it comes to maintaining her property?**

    a. Being lazy
    b. Intentionally causing harm
    c. Not abiding by community codes
    d. Being negligent

**33. Which government-funded program was established to help protect against the losses caused by flooding and aid in the recovery from natural disasters such as hurricanes?**

    a. Federal Emergency Management Agency (FEMA)
    b. Federal Flood Relief (FFR)
    c. National Flood Relief (NFR)
    d. Government Disaster Recovery (GDR)

**34. Jewelry, silverware, fine arts, and stamps are all pieces of personal property requiring more coverage than the unendorsed homeowner's policy can provide. What is the name of the floater, either attached to the homeowner's policy through endorsement or a stand-alone policy that provides specific protection for these types of personal property?**

    a. Personal Property Floater
    b. Personal Effects Property Floater
    c. Individual Articles Floater
    d. Personal Articles Floater

**35. Reagan owns and operates a food truck that she drives to different events each weekend. Because Reagan's truck does not operate out of a fixed location, what floater should she purchase to insure her food vendor business?**

    a. Vendor business floater
    b. Transport business floater
    c. Commercial property floater
    d. Food transport floater

36. Grace was in an automobile accident for which she was deemed at fault. She took her vehicle to the auto mechanic to be fixed following the accident. The mechanic sent Grace a $2500 bill for the repair work completed. Grace contacted her local insurance agent to see if the company would be paying the repair bill. Her agent informed her that after Grace pays $500 to the mechanic, the insurance company would then pay the remaining $2000 left on the bill. The $500 portion Grace is responsible for is known as what?

   a. Payment plan due
   b. Policy provision payment
   c. Deductible
   d. At fault penalty payment

37. Maria had her auto insurance policy through ABC Insurance Company. Maria asked to renew coverage but her company first needed to run a motor vehicle report to see if Maria had any violations or accidents over the past year. Her MVR came back showing three new accidents over the past year and ABC would not be able to write a policy with that many accidents. What formal notice would ABC send to Maria to notify her it would not be able to offer her renewal terms?

   a. Conditional renewal notice
   b. Non-renewal notice
   c. Loss policy release form
   d. Direct notice of cancellation

38. Why, when strict liability is applied, does negligence not need to be proven?

   a. Because the insured was involved in an act which was inherently dangerous
   b. Because the insured had no way of knowing there was danger present
   c. Negligence does need to be proven, despite the known danger.
   d. Negligence does need to be proven, due to the nature of the act.

39. Mary and Bruce have a 5-year-old son named Henry. Henry was playing baseball outside one day with his friends and threw a ball into their neighbor's window. The window shattered and glass went into the house causing additional damage. Because of Henry's age, Mary and Bruce were held responsible for paying for the damages to the neighbor's house. What type of liability is imposed on Mary and Bruce with regard to Henry's actions?

   a. Absolute liability
   b. Strict liability
   c. Parental liability
   d. Vicarious liability

40. Potential insureds go to their local insurance agents to obtain coverage to best suit their needs. Agents have their insureds fill out all the necessary paperwork, such as applications, in order to secure coverage. The agent may issue a temporary notice of coverage until the policy can be fully written and issued. What is the temporary notice of coverage called?

   a. The endorsement
   b. The binder
   c. The policy decs
   d. The policy preview

**41.** Beverly had an insurance policy written through ABC Insurance. Beverly decided about three months into the policy that she no longer wished to have coverage through ABC and found another carrier. Beverly asked ABC Insurance to cancel her policy and return the unearned premium to her attention. ABC did cancel but returned less premium than Beverly expected to get. What method did ABC use in determining how much premium to return to Beverly?

   a. Pro rata method
   b. Premium return mid-term method
   c. Short rate method
   d. Penalty rate method

**42.** Zander recently had his third accident within the past year. His insurance company was notified of the additional accident and decided to cancel Zander's policy. What method of cancellation will Zander's insurance carrier use to cancel his policy?

   a. Pro rata method
   b. Premium return mid-term method
   c. Short rate method
   d. Penalty rate method

**43.** Terrence went to his local insurance agent to obtain a homeowners policy for his newly purchased home. Terrence met all the insurance company's guidelines to be eligible for a policy except that he had an unfenced pool. The agent offered Terrence a policy but attached a document that specifically excluded the pool exposure. What is the name of the document Terrence's agent added to make Terrence's home acceptable for coverage?

   a. An endorsement
   b. A binder
   c. An exclusion clause
   d. An exemption

**44.** A car with four passengers was involved in a car accident that resulted in all four individuals needing care at the hospital. Which part of the insurance policy would cover the care provided at the hospital?

   a. The policy provisions
   b. The policy conditions
   c. Bodily injury aggregate
   d. Medical payments coverage

**45.** Insurance policies provide coverage against several forms of employee crime. What is the type of crime in which theft of property occurs with the use of force or weapons?

   a. Burglary
   b. Robbery
   c. Criminal mischief
   d. Force criminal theft

46. An example of crime coverage that is provided by some insurance policies is coverage for when a person unlawfully enters a property and steals from this property. What is this unlawful entry and theft known as?

   a. Robbery
   b. Criminal mischief
   c. Burglary
   d. Force criminal theft

47. The declarations page is often the first page of the insurance contract. On the declarations page, there is a section that names the person or group of people the contract is providing coverage for. What is the name given to the person or the group of people being afforded this coverage?

   a. The guarantor
   b. The insurer
   c. The policy provider
   d. The insured

48. Under the Terrorism Risk Insurance Act (TRIA) of 2002, which party is responsible for providing coverage against covered terrorist acts?

   a. The federal government
   b. The state government
   c. Commercial insurance carriers
   d. The local government

49. A commercial crime policy covers against losses due to employee dishonesty. Employee dishonesty protects against theft of securities, money, and which other exposure?

   a. Property
   b. Unauthorized entry
   c. Theft of company time
   d. Other employee's personal effects

50. Errors and omissions insurance is an insurance product that provides protection for claims made against professionals for what type of actions?

   a. Unintentional misrepresentation
   b. Negligent acts
   c. Failure to renew coverage
   d. Slander

51. Errors and omissions insurance covers which costs when the insured is faced with a covered claim?

   a. Defense costs
   b. Settlement costs
   c. Both court costs and settlement amount despite the policy limit
   d. Both court costs and settlement amount up to the policy limit

**52.** Medical malpractice is coverage available for professionals in the medical field such as doctors, surgeons, physicians, etc., to protect against claims of negligence by persons while in the professional's care. What statute of limitations is placed on medical malpractice claims?

    a. Two years
    b. Three years
    c. Five years
    d. Depends on the individual state the claim is filed in

**53.** Directors and officers liability insurance is a form of professional lines insurance which provides coverage for directors and officers working for all the following entities EXCEPT

    a. non-profit organizations.
    b. for-profit organizations.
    c. government entities.
    d. private firms.

**54.** Directors and officers liability insurance coverage excludes coverage for property damage and what other possible exposure?

    a. Bodily injury
    b. Financial loss
    c. Monetary damages
    d. D&O does not exclude property damage coverage.

**55.** Directors and officers liability insurance, like other insurance products, states a limit that the policy will pay up to in the event of a claim. Shrinking limits is a term used in the insurance industry to describe which costs that reduce the amount of limits available to pay the settlement?

    a. Punitive damages
    b. Defense costs
    c. Compensatory damages
    d. Appeal costs

**56.** Employment practices liability policies can be written as stand-alone or as a combined policy with a D&O policy. What is one disadvantage to having an employment practices liability policy added by endorsement to a D&O policy?

    a. Broader scope of coverage
    b. Higher cost to add coverage as opposed to two separate policies
    c. Limits may be exhausted on the combined policy due to non–D&O claims.
    d. More work on the agent to combine policies

**57.** Proximate cause is the means to determine the cause of loss. Proximate cause says that which peril is the one responsible for the loss that occurred?

    a. The peril that occurred second in the chain leading to the loss
    b. All perils that lead to the loss are said to be the proximate cause of loss.
    c. The first peril that lead to the loss
    d. The peril that is most directly associated with the loss

**58.** Howard was at his son's baseball game when a foul ball was hit into the parking lot. The ball crashed through Howard's windshield and shattered the entire window. Howard had his car towed to his mechanic and submitted a claim under his auto insurance policy. What coverage would Howard need to have in order for coverage to apply?

   a. Collision coverage
   b. Other-than-collision coverage
   c. Incidental accident coverage
   d. Accidental damage coverage

**59.** What type of automobile insurance will provide coverage when the auto is in an accident with another vehicle or collides with an object, such as a road sign or guard rail?

   a. Collision coverage
   b. Other-than-collision coverage
   c. Incidental accident coverage
   d. Accidental damage coverage

**60.** The limits on an insurance policy can be presented in multiple forms. Which form indicates that a single dollar limit applies to the policy?

   a. Combined single limit
   b. Split limits
   c. Per person limit
   d. Per occurrence limit

**61.** An insurance policy can have its policy limits represented by a single limit or by split limits. A policy that uses split limits to indicate the amount of coverage available typically shows how many split limits?

   a. Five limits
   b. Two limits
   c. Four limits
   d. Three limits

**62.** Frankie was involved in a car accident and deemed at fault. He hit an elderly woman who needed to seek medical care over a long-term basis from injuries caused by the accident. If Frankie's auto policy was written with the split limit approach, which limit would respond to pay toward the woman's extensive medical care?

   a. Limit two
   b. Limit one
   c. Limit three
   d. Limits one and three

**63.** If an insured has an auto policy that uses the split limits approach, which limit will indicate the maximum policy limit allowed for property damage?

   a. Limit two
   b. Limit one
   c. Limit three
   d. There is no available limit for property damage under the split limits approach.

64. Automobile insurance is a requirement in every state. While it is a requirement by law, often individuals do not obtain insurance due to its cost or because they do not think they need insurance. For those who do have proper insurance, what coverage is important to protect yourself in case you are involved in an accident where the at-fault party does not carry insurance?

    a. Non-insured motorist coverage
    b. Extra care coverage
    c. Uninsured motorist coverage
    d. Replacement insurance coverage

65. Underinsured motorist coverage is coverage available when the at-fault party to an accident has insurance but not sufficient limits to cover possible claims. Underinsured motorist coverage will apply, when written with limits trigger, if liability limits carried by the at-fault party are lower or higher than the underinsured limits the insured has?

    a. Higher
    b. Lower
    c. The same
    d. Depends on the severity of the claim

66. Bill was planning a road trip for his family's annual vacation. Bill did not want to drive his own vehicle as it was older and in need of some repairs. Bill decided to rent a vehicle to make the trip and called his insurance agent to see if this rented vehicle would have coverage under his automobile policy. Will the vehicle Bill is renting have coverage under his automobile insurance policy?

    a. No, rentals are always excluded.
    b. No, rentals for the purpose of family personal use are excluded.
    c. Yes, but he would have to pay additional premiums regardless of what type of policy he has.
    d. Yes, his rental vehicle would be considered a "hired auto" and will have coverage as a temporary auto.

67. Under a commercial auto policy, what coverage is afforded to vehicles the named insured does not own but that employees are using during the course of business?

    a. Nonowned automobile
    b. Employee automobile
    c. Newly acquired automobile
    d. Company automobile

68. Norman recently purchased an additional automobile to be used by his 16-year-old son. Does Norman need to tell his insurance company about the newly purchased vehicle?

    a. No, coverage applies to any and all autos purchased by the insured regardless of whether the insurance company is aware of the vehicle.
    b. Yes, insurance companies specify the time frame in which a newly acquired auto needs to be added to the policy for adequate coverage to exist for the auto.
    c. Yes, insurance companies must be informed the day the auto is purchased or else there is no coverage for the new vehicle.
    d. No, they just need to tell the company at renewal regardless of at what point in the policy period the vehicle is purchased.

69. Reid was involved in a car accident but was not at fault. The damage to his vehicle required extensive work and he would be without his car for a couple of weeks. Reid obtained a rental car during the time his own car was being fixed. What endorsement does Reid need to have on his automobile policy to be reimbursed for the rental car?

   a. Drive other car endorsement
   b. Rental reimbursement coverage endorsement
   c. Rental car endorsement
   d. Replacement car reimbursement endorsement

70. A garagekeepers coverage is designed for insureds who are in what business?

   a. Parking garages
   b. Garage repair
   c. Garage storage
   d. Auto and trailer dealers

71. What type of coverage extends the liability coverage available under the garagekeepers coverage policy?

   a. Garagekeepers extended coverage
   b. Garagekeepers additional coverage
   c. Garagekeepers extra legal liability
   d. Garagekeepers add-on liability

72. Following a court ruling on a claim, what damages may be awarded to the plaintiff for pain and suffering?

   a. General damages
   b. Punitive damages
   c. Special damages
   d. Tangible damages

73. What damages awarded by a court are to compensate the injured person for expenses such as loss of wages and medical expenses?

   a. General damages
   b. Punitive damages
   c. Special damages
   d. Tangible damages

74. Brent was the beneficiary named on his parent's life insurance policy. His parents passed away suddenly from an accident, and Brent received a lump sum of money from the life insurance carrier. What is the amount of money Brent received known as?

   a. Policy payment
   b. Death benefit
   c. Beneficiary payment
   d. Policy payout

75. Punitive damages are a monetary award given to a plaintiff to punish a defendant for negligent or intentional actions. The majority of umbrella policies exclude coverage for punitive damages, but what two types of insurance policies usually do not exclude punitive damages?

   a. Excess liability and commercial general liability policies
   b. Excess liability and business auto policies
   c. Commercial general liability and personal auto policies
   d. Commercial general liability and business auto policies

76. If an employer fails to obtain proper insurance for its company and employees, would the employees be allowed to file a tort claim in the event of an injury?

   a. No, the bar to file a tort claim is only lifted if there was willful negligence regardless of the insurance obtained.
   b. Yes, if there was willful negligence on the part of the employer as well.
   c. Yes, regardless of the employer's role in the injury the bar against filing a tort claim would be lifted.
   d. No, the bar is never lifted to allow employees to file a tort claim against the employer.

77. Dwelling polices and homeowner's policies are often confused as being the same coverage. Name one difference between the two types of policies.

   a. Homeowners policies, despite the name, do not require the dwelling to be owner occupied.
   b. Dwelling policies cover theft on every policy written.
   c. Dwelling policies do not have to be for owner occupied residences.
   d. Homeowners policies do not cover theft automatically.

78. In cases of a multi-family dwelling, how many of the units must be occupied by the named insured to be eligible for a homeowner's policy?

   a. 1
   b. 2
   c. 3
   d. 0

79. The dwelling policy is currently written on three different forms: DP-1, DP-2, and DP-3. Which of the three dwelling forms is written on an open perils basis?

   a. DP-1
   b. DP-2
   c. DP-3
   d. None of the dwelling forms is written on an open perils basis.

80. Edmund purchased a new home that included 120 acres of farmland and a barn. Edmund's plan was to start growing crops on his farm and sell to the public as his main source of income. Which dwelling policy should Edmund obtain to cover his needs?

   a. DP-1
   b. DP-2
   c. DP-3
   d. None of the dwelling policies can provide coverage for farming exposures.

81. Aircrafts provide a unique and uncommon risk to homeowners. Which dwelling policy provides automatic coverage from damage that may occur from an object falling off of an aircraft?

   a. DP-1
   b. DP-2
   c. DP-3
   d. All dwelling policies exclude all risks associated with aircrafts.

82. ABC Insurance learned of a large tornado heading in the direction of a local town. Calls started coming into ABC asking for new property policies and an increase in property limits to existing policies. ABC Insurance issued a statement that it would not write new policies or increase policy limits for a limited period of time. This attempt was to stop the public from purchasing property policies only because there was the risk of an excessive loss to their property. What situation was ABC faced with due to the threat of the tornado?

   a. Increased threat to the public
   b. Adverse selection
   c. Severity exposure
   d. Policy discrimination

83. When reviewing your personal insurance policy, which section should you closely review to see any and all potential exposures you would not be insured against?

   a. The policy provisions
   b. The declaration
   c. The exclusions
   d. The endorsements

84. Which section of the insurance policy will specify that the insurance company will make payment on approved claims?

   a. The insuring agreement
   b. The policy declarations
   c. The exclusions
   d. The endorsements

85. Marty's vehicle was involved in a three-car accident. The accident left Marty's vehicle no longer usable, and the insurance company declared the vehicle a total loss. Even though the vehicle is inoperable, parts of the vehicle could be used by a scrap yard or mechanic shop. What value is given to the parts of Marty's vehicle that are still usable?

   a. Rec value
   b. Service value
   c. Salvage value
   d. Reconstruction value

86. Which form of homeowner's policy is designed to cover the tenants of the insured dwelling on a named perils basis?

   a. HO-2
   b. HO-3
   c. HO-4
   d. HO-6

**87. A commercial package policy (CPP) is an insurance policy for businesses which combines coverage for property and what other coverage into one policy?**

a. Auto
b. Professional
c. D&O
d. Liability

**88. In an office building, furniture, fixtures, and computers are all different forms of what type of property?**

a. Business tangible property
b. Business personal property
c. Commercial property
d. Executive property

**89. Amber was in the process of applying for a new job as a computer specialist. The company Amber was applying to ran a credit report without first gaining Amber's written consent. Was it legal for this company to run her credit report without written consent?**

a. No, a company is required to obtain written consent prior to running a credit report.
b. No, a company is only allowed to run credit reports for specific lines of work, and computer specialist is not included in that list.
c. Yes, a company can run a credit report without consent.
d. Yes, a company is protected by the Fair Credit Reporting Act and can run a credit report on any potential employee.

**90. Robert was in the process of obtaining a pre-approval for a mortgage on a home he was planning to purchase. Robert wanted to know his credit score but was too impatient to wait for the loan company to return his phone calls. Can Robert request his credit score on his own?**

a. Yes, but he will have to pay for it.
b. Yes, and his loan company will be billed for it.
c. No, only the mortgage company can request a credit score.
d. No, the credit bureau will not release scores to individuals, only to licensed businesses.

**91. Suzanna was reviewing her credit report as she was sitting in her mortgage lender's office. She noticed a discrepancy on her report for being charged late fees for a credit card she did not even own. Is Suzanna allowed to dispute this error on her credit report?**

a. No, disputes are not allowed in any case.
b. No, only mortgage companies can file a dispute for you.
c. Yes, but there is a minimum dollar amount of charges against her that must be met in order to dispute.
d. Yes, you can dispute information that is inaccurate.

**92. After winning a dispute from the credit bureau over inaccurate information, how long does the credit bureau have to correct the information on the credit report?**

a. 1 week
b. 60 days
c. 30 days
d. 90 days

93. **Which act was designed around the need for insurance companies and banking companies to consolidate for the better good of the economy?**
   a. The Fair Consumer Act
   b. The Gramm Leach Bliley Act
   c. The Gramm Clinton Act
   d. The Leach Clinton Act

94. **Hunter had an insurance policy through ABC Insurance that just ended last month. Hunter forgot to report a claim to his insurance carrier and was wondering if he was still able to report the claim. What type of policy must Hunter have had to be able to report his claim?**
   a. Occurrence
   b. Claims-made
   c. Extension endorsement
   d. Lag policy

95. **First aid expenses, pre-judgment interest, and required travel expenses are all expenses an insured may incur after a claim. These bills may be reimbursed to the insured by the insurance company through what type of payments?**
   a. Judgment payments
   b. Defense costs
   c. Insured costs
   d. Supplemental payments

96. **With regard to supplemental payments, how do professional liability policies differ from commercial general liability (CGL) policies?**
   a. Professional policy limits are often reduced by the supplemental payments.
   b. Commercial general liability (CGL) policy limits are often reduced by the supplemental payments.
   c. Professional policies exclude supplemental payments.
   d. Commercial general liability policies only cover supplemental payments if there is a specific endorsement attached.

97. **Bob is the owner of a large company that is in need of some repairs to its office building. Bob was interviewing contractors in the area and one of his requirements was proof they had sufficient insurance coverage in place. What form may these contractors present to Bob to provide proof of their insurance policies?**
   a. The entire policy
   b. Written letter from insurance company
   c. Certificate of insurance
   d. A company does not have to provide proof of insurance by the Gramm Leach Bliley Act.

98. **Before an insurance company can determine if it will cover a loss, what must the insured provide?**
   a. Proof of loss
   b. Signed copy of the application
   c. Proof of repairs
   d. Signed statement of loss control measures

99. Insurance applications require the potential policyholders to be completely accurate and honest with their answers. When a potential insured holds back information that could be considered relevant to the type of insurance being provided, this is known as what act?

   a. Fraud
   b. Lying
   c. Concealment
   d. Minor crime

100. Which category of hazards results from damage by the insured's business operations while the operations are occurring on the Insured's premises?

   a. Products-completed operations
   b. Premises-operations
   c. Moral
   d. Physical location

101. Like premises-operations, products-completed operations provides coverage for liability caused by the insured's business operations. However, for products-completed operations, where does the loss have to take place?

   a. At the insured's premises
   b. Within five miles of the insured's premises
   c. While still in the control of the insured
   d. Away from the insured's premises

102. Earthquake coverage is usually excluded on all property policies except for what exposure associated with earthquakes?

   a. Earth movement
   b. Ensuing fire
   c. Collapse
   d. Tree damage

103. Katherine is wishing to obtain coverage for her manufactured home. Does Katherine need to get an endorsed homeowners policy, regular homeowners policy, or a stand-alone mobile home policy?

   a. An endorsed homeowner's policy
   b. Regular homeowner's policy
   d. A stand-alone mobile home policy
   d. An endorsed homeowners or stand-alone mobile home policy

104. Property insurance policies often contain mortgagee clauses. If the insured commits an act which causes the policy to be voided, will the mortgagee still be provided coverage for the location on the policy?

   a. Yes, but the mortgagee in turn will take on all the responsibilities the insured previously held as owner of the policy.
   b. Yes, and any outstanding premium due is erased.
   c. No, the policy is voided for all parties.
   d. No, the policy must be rewritten with the consent of the previous insured.

**105. Financial institutions have what requirement for an insurance policy prior to offering large loans?**
   a. Proof of funds
   b. Signed statements
   c. Mortgagee clause
   d. Proof of no property liens

**106. The wind and hail deductible is often added to policies written for locations where there is a higher chance of loss due to wind and hail. Is this deductible always a specific dollar amount?**
   a. Yes.
   b. Yes, unless a special additional endorsement is added to amend the deductible amount.
   c. No, it may be a specific dollar amount or a percentage of the property value.
   d. No, it is always a percentage of the property value.

**107. Farmowners insurance is a specialized form of insurance that provides what type(s) of coverage?**
   a. Homeowner's
   b. Commercial property
   c. Commercial liability coverage
   d. Homeowners, commercial property, and commercial liability coverage

**108. Why are farmowners insurance policies a combination of homeowners, commercial property, and commercial liability policies?**
   a. To avoid writing three separate policies
   b. Because farms have commercial as well as residential characteristics
   c. Farmowners does not offer a combined policy and rather has three separate policies to make sure all exposures are covered.
   d. To give the insured a premium break as opposed to three separate policies

**109. The federal government has insurance programs available for crop insurance. Does the federal government's crop program cover damage by hail?**
   a. No, this is purchased through licensed insurance agents.
   b. No, hail coverage is not available for crops.
   c. Yes, but just through an additional endorsement
   d. Yes, on the standard policy

**110. Which other perils can be added to crop-hail insurance?**
   a. Wind
   b. Collapse
   c. Fire
   d. Wind and fire

**111.** Martha is interested in obtaining business income coverage to cover her business in the event a loss occurs and the business is shut down for some time. Martha has some questions for her agent, including whether or not coverage would end as soon as the repairs from a loss are made?

    a. Yes, the policy ends once repairs are complete.
    b. No, coverage will extend a specific number of days.
    c. Yes, only in the event of catastrophe could coverage be extended.
    d. No, coverage will last for the remainder of the policy period.

**112.** Under any circumstances is an insured allowed to transfer an insurance contract to another party?

    a. No, under no circumstances
    b. Yes, without consent
    c. Yes, with the insured's consent
    d. Yes, with the insurer's consent

**113.** Subrogation is the insurance process of one party, the insurer, stepping in for the responsible party to indemnify the insured for their loss. The insurer then tries to recoup, or subrogate, from the responsible party. Why would subrogation ever be waived?

    a. Subrogation is never allowed to be waived.
    b. To penalize the insurer if there was any wrongdoing on its part
    c. To prevent or lessen the likelihood of lawsuits
    d. If all parties agree to waive

**114.** Matt worked as an insurance agent for ABC Insurance. He was in the process of trying to place coverage for a potential policyholder. Matt asked the potential client to provide a completed application and consent to pull motor vehicle reports and a credit report. What information was Matt collecting?

    a. Sources of underwriting information
    b. Future claims notes
    c. Information for reinsurance purposes
    d. Information to compare to other policyholders

**115.** Determining an automobile's fair market value is often used to determine what other value placed on the auto?

    a. Replacement cost
    b. Actual cash value
    c. Salvage value
    d. Insured value

**116.** After a loss, the insured has the duty to notify the insurance company in a timely manner for coverage to apply. All of the following are other duties the insured has when a loss occurs EXCEPT

    a. to fix the loss independently.
    b. to try to prevent further damage to the property.
    c. to provide proof of the loss.
    d. to submit any signed statements the insurance company may require following the loss.

**117.** Bodily injury is a coverage afforded by many insurance policies. Bodily injury includes all the following EXCEPT
    a. sickness.
    b. death.
    c. bodily harm.
    d. slander.

**118.** Is tail coverage automatically attached to all policies at no extra cost to the insured?
    a. Yes, in all cases
    b. No, it is added only by endorsement but at no cost.
    c. No, it is added to claims-made policies at an additional cost.
    d. No, it is added to occurrence-triggered policies at an additional cost.

**119.** Ryan has an insurance policy through ABC Insurance for September 1, 2008, through September 1, 2009. His policy contains a runoff provision for a five-year term. If a claim was submitted against Ryan on September 2, 2015, for a loss occurring on June 1, 2009, would Ryan's insurance policy cover the loss?
    a. Yes, because the loss occurred during the policy period.
    b. Yes, because the claim was reported only shortly after the runoff period.
    c. No, because the claim was reported after the runoff period.
    d. No, because the loss must occur during the runoff period as well.

**120.** Claims-made and occurrence are known as what with regard to an insurance policy?
    a. The cause of loss
    b. The method of payment
    c. The coverage triggers
    d. The premium triggers

# Answer Key and Explanations

**1. B:** The guarantor. The guarantor, or the surety, is the party that guarantees the contract will be fulfilled in its entirety to the guarantee. The guarantor can require another party to join its role in ensuring the contract is fulfilled if the guarantor needs to lower the risk involved with the account.

**2. A:** The principal. The principal is the party responsible in the surety bond contract for performing the actual work being insured. The principal is performing this work for the obligee and the guarantor is guaranteeing the principal will perform the work to fulfill the contract.

**3. C:** Fidelity bonds cannot be traded. A fidelity bond is different from a regular bond in two ways. A fidelity bond is not able to be traded like a regular bond, and a fidelity bond is not able to accrue interest. A fidelity bond's purpose is to serve only as an insurance policy and does not hold additional functions.

**4. A:** Coinsurance clause. A coinsurance clause is a requirement on some insurance contracts to make sure the insured is insuring his exposures at adequate limits. A coinsurance clause will typically require 80% of the value of the dwelling to be covered for coverage to be valid. The intent of this clause is to ensure the policyholder is carrying enough limits should a loss occur, rather than just purchasing a policy at minimal limits to satisfy the state requirement of having a policy.

**5. D:** An insurable interest in the exposure. A potential policyholder must have an insurable interest in the exposure for which insurance coverage is needed. Insurable interest means that should there be a loss to this exposure; the insured would suffer the consequences of that loss.

**6. B:** Law of large numbers. The law of large numbers concept believes that the larger the sample size, the more the average of data collected will be closer to the expected value. The law of large numbers is a means of collecting data to confirm the result expected is the actual result from a true sample of real exposures.

**7. D:** Speculative risk. A speculative risk is a risk in which the insured can either lose or gain from the risk. By purchasing the stocks, Scott runs the risk of losing money but also runs the chance of gaining money as well.

**8. A:** Pure risk. Simon is taking on a pure risk by purchasing his new car. A pure risk is a risk in which there is no chance of a gain, just the chance of a loss occurring. A pure risk is always undesirable as there is no potential for a monetary gain.

**9. C:** Local city government. Local city governments, as well as county and state governments, will often require proof of insurance through a builder's risk policy as part of their contract with the construction company performing the work. This insurance policy protects against perils such as fire, wind, and vandalism.

**10. C:** Theft. Builder's risk insurance typically will exclude such exposures as wind in coastal areas, earthquake, and flood. Builder's risk insurance does usually cover the theft exposure, as well as wind in noncoastal regions and fire. This coverage will only apply during the course of construction and will terminate once construction is complete.

**11. B:** Lost wages from employees not being able to work. The building damage, sidewalk repair, and roof leaking are all direct losses associated with the hurricane. The employees losing their wages is an indirect loss of the business not being able to operate during the repair period after the hurricane. The hurricane did not cause the wages to not be paid but rather caused the building to be closed and therefore wages are not able to be paid.

**12. B:** Damage to her roof requiring repair. Kendall's house sustained the direct loss to her roof from the tropical storm. Kendall's increased cost of the hotel and food are an indirect loss associated with the damage caused by the tropical storm. Kendall's inconvenience in her commute is also indirectly caused by the storm but is not a direct loss.

**13. A:** Age hazard. Moral, morale and physical hazards are all hazards that concern insurance companies as they assume risks. Each of these hazards, if present, can increase the chance a risk will occur as well possibly increase the payout needed to settle the risk. Age is not necessarily a hazard but rather a characteristic of a risk. Most states, with respect to age of operators, prohibit discrimination against the age of applicants requesting insurance.

**14. D:** Physical hazard. Peter has created a physical hazard by not properly cleaning up the debris on his sidewalk. This physical hazard presents the chance of trip and fall, debris blowing into the street, and other means of causing damage. This physical hazard has increased Peter's chances of a loss occurring.

**15. C:** Morale hazard. A morale hazard exists when an insured no longer tries to protect his exposures to the best of his ability because he is just relying on insurance to cover the loss. Part of an insurance agreement is that the insured will act with reasonable care in protecting his exposures to the best of his ability. A morale hazard breaks this agreement and relies solely on the insurance company to pay for the loss.

**16. A:** Moral hazard. Brenton committed a moral hazard by knowingly lying about his credit history in order to benefit from obtaining an insurance contract. An insurance contract requires all parties to enter in good faith, and therefore the contract may be voided if the carrier were to find out Brenton lied on the application.

**17. D:** Policy exclusions. The declarations page, or dec page, contains the named insured, policy limits, premises being covered, and the policy period. The exclusions pertaining to the policy are not found on the declarations page but rather in their own section of the policy.

**18. B:** The insuring agreement. The insuring agreement is the section of the insurance policy that states the hazards the policy intends to cover, the parties covered by the policy, and how long the contract will be in force. The insuring agreement does not typically touch on exclusions that pertain to the specific policy as exclusions have their own section in the contract.

**19. C:** Policy conditions. The policy conditions section of an insurance policy will indicate what will happen should a coverage change be required during the policy term. The policy conditions section also covers cancellation, inspections, and assignment of the insurance policy.

**20. D:** Policy exclusions. The policy exclusions section of an insurance policy will state what exclusions apply for specific exposures, locations, or acts. This provision is important because the insured may believe he has full coverage for exposures, such as Terrance did, but this section takes away some of the coverage.

**21. A:** Actual cash value. Actual cash value is determined by subtracting the depreciation from the replacement cost value of a specific piece of property. The insured does not prefer actual cash value as a method of payment from the insurance company because more money would be paid if the property were assessed at replacement cost.

**22. D:** Replacement cost. Replacement cost valuation requires an insurance company to replace property with the same or equal value in the event of a loss. This is ideal for the insured as opposed to actual cash value, which subtracts depreciation from the replacement cost value.

**23. A:** Special form. Inventory storage, unauthorized instructions, and employee dishonesty are some examples of theft exclusions under policies containing the special form cause of loss. Some other theft exclusions include unexplained disappearance, building material theft, and voluntary parting.

**24. B:** Yes, broad form does include coverage due to the weight causing the roof to collapse. Roof coverage is available in this case as the damage was caused from weight due to snow and sleet. Broad form also may provide coverage for all perils insured under basic form as well as falling objects; collapse; and weight of sleet, ice, and snow.

**25. C:** Lightning. Lightning is a peril already included under the basic form cause of loss and not an addition due to broad form. Basic form also provides coverage for loss from hail, sprinkler leakage, riot, fire, smoke, etc. Broad form will add additional perils such as falling objects; collapse; and weight from ice, snow, and sleet.

**26. C:** HO-4. An HO-4 policy is a type of homeowners policy designed for a tenant of a location who does not have ownership in the building itself. The HO-4 will provide protection for the tenant's personal property but does not provide coverage for the dwelling.

**27. B:** HO-5. The HO-5 comprehensive form provides coverage for the dwelling, personal property, and other structures on an all risks basis. The HO-5 is the broadest homeowners form available for owner-occupied dwellings.

**28. D:** Broad form. An HO-2 policy form provides coverage for the dwelling on a broad form cause of loss basis. The HO-2 also provides for medical payments and personal liability coverage, in addition to coverage on the dwelling itself and other structures.

**29. A:** Unscheduled personal property. Unscheduled personal property is covered on a broad named perils basis under an HO-3 policy form. The dwelling, other structures, and scheduled personal property are all covered on an all risk basis. Medical payments and personal liability are also provided by the HO-3 policy.

**30. B:** Provides less property coverage than the HO-3. The HO-6 provides less property coverage because it is not designed to be the only policy covering the common areas or structures shared by the condominium community. The HO-6 protects the condominium unit owners for their personal units and personal property. To have coverage over shared exposures, another policy should be in place to cover the unique needs of shared spaces or structures.

**31. C:** Basic form. The HO-8 modified homeowners form protects against perils on a basic named perils basis. The HO-8 is used for homes in which the replacement cost may be higher than the market value due to the materials or methods needed to restore historic homes.

**32. D:** Being negligent. Margaret was negligent when it came to shoveling her driveway after the ice storm. Negligence is failure to act in a way a reasonable person would act. A reasonable person would have shoveled the sidewalk to prevent injury.

**33. A:** Federal Emergency Management Agency (FEMA). FEMA is a government-funded agency started in 1979 to help prepare for, respond to, and aid in the recovery from natural disasters.

FEMA not only will support citizens affected by the disasters, but also helps to aid first responders in their efforts to respond to such natural disasters.

**34. D:** Personal articles floater. The personal articles floater is designed to provide coverage in addition to the limited coverage a homeowners policy affords for scheduled personal property. Such property can include stamps, jewelry, silverware, fine arts, furs, cameras, etc. This floater can be added through endorsement to a homeowners policy.

**35. C:** Commercial property floater. Reagan should purchase a commercial property floater to insure her food truck property exposure. This floater is added by endorsement to a property insurance policy and is specifically designed to cover business exposures that do not operate at one fixed location.

**36. C:** Deductible. Grace, under her insurance contract, is responsible for a $200 deductible toward any claims submitted. If the claim exceeds $200, the insurance company will step in after the $200 deductible is paid to pay the rest of the bill up to the policy limit.

**37. B:** Non-renewal notice. ABC Insurance Company would be required to send Maria a formal non-renewal notice if it were not able to offer renewal terms. Each state has specific time frames in which non-renewal notices must be sent before the policy expires to provide the insured with enough time to secure coverage elsewhere.

**38. A:** Because the insured was involved in an act which was inherently dangerous. Strict or absolute liability is present when the insured enters a situation in which there is an inherent or known danger. An example would be the insured entering the cage of a wild animal such as a mountain lion. The insured knows the mountain lion is dangerous and still enters the cage despite the risk involved.

**39. D:** Vicarious liability. Mary and Bruce would be held vicariously liable for Henry's actions due to his being a child and not able to indemnify the neighbors for their loss. The parents are supposed to be in charge of Henry, and if he is negligent, the parents need to be held liable.

**40. B:** The binder. A binder is a temporary document stating insurance coverage was secured. The binder serves just as a temporary document while the agent or underwriter collects all necessary paperwork to issue a full policy. Once the policy is issued, the binder is no longer valid.

**41. C:** Short rate method. ABC Insurance determined the return amount Beverly was owed based on the short rate method. This method imposes a penalty on the insured for cancelling the policy to place coverage with a competitor.

**42. A:** Pro rata method. Zander's insurance company would refund any unearned premium on a pro rata basis. The pro rata method does not punish the insured because, as in Zander's case, the insurance company was the party cancelling the contract, not Zander.

**43. A:** An endorsement. Terrence's agent was able to add an endorsement to exclude the pool and therefore make Terrence a fit for their insurance product. An endorsement makes an amendment to a policy, typically by adding or taking away coverage the stand-alone policy allows.

**44. D:** Medical payments coverage. The medical payments coverage stated on your auto insurance policy is the part of the policy that responds when the insured driver and any passengers need medical attention immediately following an accident. The medical payments coverage will respond regardless of fault if care is sought immediately following the accident.

**45. B:** Robbery. Robbery is a type of crime many insurance companies offer coverage for. Robbery is theft, like burglary, but the theft occurs with weapons or force. The force can be actually used or it can be implied, where the victim felt threatened by force.

**46. C:** Burglary. Burglary is a form of crime that is covered against by many insurance companies. Burglary involves a theft by unlawfully entering a premises and stealing from that premises. Burglary, unlike robbery, does not involve force or weapons used against another individual.

**47. D:** The insured. The insured is the person, group of people, or party that the insurance policy is providing coverage for. The insured is always named on the declarations page of the policy. While being the party afforded the coverage, the insured is also the party responsible for all policy premiums and for following all policy conditions.

**48. C:** Commercial insurance carriers. The Terrorism Risk Insurance Act of 2002 requires that commercial insurance carriers provide coverage against covered acts of terrorism. The insurance company is then reimbursed for its payments by the federal government, subject to a deductible amount.

**49. A:** Property. Employee dishonesty in a commercial crime policy protects against theft of property, securities, and money. Employee dishonesty is written on a per-loss, per-employee, or per-position limit.

**50. B:** Negligent acts. Errors and omissions coverage protects a professional against a claim due to negligent acts. Errors and omissions coverage is often a requirement by government regulatory groups in order for the insured to work in a professional environment.

**51. D:** Both court costs and settlement amount up to the policy limit. Errors and omissions not only will cover settlement amounts for covered claims but also will provide court costs within the policy limits. Errors and omissions coverage can be provided by a stand-alone policy or through endorsement to a commercial policy.

**52. D:** Depends on the individual state the claim is filed in. Each state's common law system sets a limited time, or statute, in which a medical malpractice claim can be filed. The statute's purpose is to prevent fraudulent claims from coming in well after the incident occurred.

**53. C:** Government entities. Directors and officers liability insurance provides coverage for for-profit, non-profit, and private firms' directors and officers. This type of insurance provides coverage against claims that the directors' or officers' decision resulted in a financial loss.

**54. A:** Bodily injury. Directors and officers liability insurance does not provide coverage for claims made for property damage or bodily injury claims. D&O coverage does, however, provide coverage for monetary damages charged against the insureds for their acts while in their professional environment.

**55. B:** Defense costs. Defense costs are included in the limit the directors and officers policy states, not in addition to the limits. Defense costs are said to be "shrinking limits" because they lower the amount of limits available to pay the settlement owed to the party making the claim.

**56. C:** Limits may be exhausted on the combined policy due to non-D&O claims. When you combine two different coverages, such as employment practices liability and D&O, you only offer one limit to cover essentially two products. When multiple claims come in under the employment practices coverage, the limits left for possible D&O claims are severely limited.

**57. D:** The peril which is most directly associated with the loss. Multiple perils may be involved in causing a loss to occur. The peril which is determined to be most directly associated with the loss is known as the proximate cause of that same loss.

**58. B:** Other-than-collision coverage. Howard would need to have other-than-collision coverage as part of his auto insurance policy in order for coverage to apply. Other-than-collision coverage protects on an "all risks" protection form for losses other than collision losses.

**59. A:** Collision coverage. Collision coverage is a form of automobile insurance which provides coverage when the vehicle is in an accident with another vehicle. Collision coverage can also step in to provide coverage when the insured's vehicle collides into objects such as guard rails, road signs, etc.

**60. A:** Combined single limit. When a policy indicates there is a combined single limit, this limit covers the possible bodily injury claims and the property damage claims. Combined single limits are noted by a single dollar limit listed on the policy, as opposed to split limits which show three-dollar limits.

**61. D:** Three limits. A policy written using split limits will show three separate limits. Limit one indicates the maximum to be paid to any one individual injured. Limit two indicates the maximum for all injured persons to be paid. Finally, limit three indicates the maximum per occurrence limit to claims involving property damage.

**62. B:** Limit one. In the split limit approach, limit one will show the maximum amount allowed to be paid to any single, injured person from the accident. Frankie's limit one of his split limits will pay towards the elderly woman's settlement request due to her being an injured party in the accident.

**63. C:** Limit three. Under a split limit policy, the third limit indicates the maximum limit available to pay per occurrence for property damage. This limit can be used to pay for damage to other autos or other forms of property damaged as a result of the accident.

**64. C:** Uninsured motorist coverage. Uninsured motorist (UM) coverage is part of your insurance policy that helps protect you in the event you are in an accident and the at-fault party does not have coverage. If the victim has uninsured motorist coverage, their own insurance will provide coverage in the absence of an insurance policy for the negligent operator.

**65. B:** Lower. Underinsured motorist coverage will apply if written with a limits trigger when the at-fault party has liability limits lower than the insured's underinsured motorist limit. The limits trigger does not depend on the severity of the claim, just the overall limits carried by the at-fault party.

**66. D:** Yes, his rental vehicle would be considered a "hired auto" and will have coverage as a temporary auto. Vehicles rented, leased, or borrowed by the insured from a rental business are afforded coverage as a hired auto. This coverage typically only applies to private passenger vehicles.

**67. A:** Nonowned automobile. Under a commercial auto policy, this is the coverage for vehicles the named insured does not own but that employees are using during the course of business. These vehicles are classified as nonowned automobiles by the policy. These nonowned autos must be private passenger vehicles for coverage to apply.

**68. B:** Yes, insurance companies specify the time frame in which a newly acquired auto needs to be added to the policy for adequate coverage to exist for the auto. Most insurance companies have a time frame in which they must be informed of new purchases for full coverage to apply. Common time frames are 30 or 60 days. Failure to notify your insurance company of a newly acquired vehicle may allow the company to limit or deny coverage for that vehicle in the event of a claim.

**69. B:** Rental reimbursement coverage endorsement. Reid needed to have the rental reimbursement coverage endorsement on his automobile insurance policy to be reimbursed for the expense of his rental vehicle. Usually the carrier will require a car of similar type and value to the car that sustained the physical damage.

**70. D:** Auto and trailer dealers. The garagekeepers coverage provides insurance for insureds who have the liability exposure of autos being left in their care to be serviced or maintained. Liability on the insured must be determined in order for coverage to apply.

**71. C:** Garagekeepers extra legal liability. Garagekeepers extra legal liability extends the liability coverage available under the garagekeepers coverage policy. Under this extra coverage, liability does not have to be determined on the part of the insured.

**72. A:** General damages. General damages are a monetary amount designated to the plaintiff for pain and suffering caused by a covered accident. General damages are a subjective amount, as a dollar amount cannot be assigned to pain and suffering.

**73. C:** Special damages. Courts award a monetary amount to compensate the injured party for expenses such as loss of wages, medical expenses, and nursing care. Special damages are not subjective, like general damages, as a dollar amount is available for each expense the injured party sustains.

**74. B:** Death benefit. Brent, as the beneficiary on his parent's life insurance policy, received a death benefit payment when his parents passed away. The death benefit is only paid out to the beneficiary once the named insured is deceased.

**75. D:** Commercial general liability and business auto policies. Standard business auto and commercial general liability policies do not specifically exclude punitive damages. Punitive damages, however, are excluded under most excess liability and umbrella policies.

**76. B:** Yes, if there was willful negligence on the part of the employer as well. The bar, which does not allow employees to file a tort claim, is lifted if there is willful negligence by the employer and the employer did not obtain adequate insurance. The employees normally are not allowed to file tort claims as they are supposed to only follow their worker's compensation benefit laws.

**77. C:** Dwelling policies do not have to be for owner occupied residences. Dwelling policies can be written to cover as a tenant's policy only and not include an owner occupied location. For a homeowner's policy, the dwelling must be occupied by the homeowner. The dwelling product also does not always include theft unless theft coverage is added through endorsement.

**78. A:** 1. In cases of a multi-family dwelling, at least one of the units must be occupied by the named insured to be eligible for a homeowner's policy. This is a main difference between homeowners and dwelling policies. The dwelling policy does not have an owner occupant location as an eligibility requirement to write the risk.

**79. C:** DP-3. The DP-3 dwelling form is the only dwelling form written on an open perils basis for the dwelling and other structures. The DP-3 provides coverage for contents on a broad form basis. The DP-1 and DP-2 are written on a named perils basis.

**80. D:** None of the dwelling policies can provide coverage for farming exposures. Edmund would not be eligible for a dwelling policy as they all list farming as an ineligible exposure. Edmund would need a more extensive policy not only to cover his needs on the premises for the farming exposures but also to cover his exposure to selling to the public.

**81. B:** DP-2. The DP-2 dwelling form will provide coverage automatically for damage caused from aircrafts making contact with the insured's dwelling or property. This could also include coverage for any damage occurring from an object falling off the aircraft and damaging the insured's property. This coverage could also be found on a DP-1 if added by endorsement.

**82. B:** Adverse selection. Adverse selection is the risk insurers face when the potential for severe damage is present. Adverse selection involves potential policyholders trying to obtain coverage only because they know a threat to their property is great. These potential policyholders should have obtained coverage all along and not just during times of high exposure. This puts the insurance company at risk for issuing large claims settlements when, after receiving the settlement money, the insureds may just cancel their policies to avoid future premium payments.

**83. C:** The exclusions. The exclusions section contains the wording for any exposure, even if listed earlier in the policy, against which the insured is not covered. The policyholder should also pay close attention to the endorsements attached to the policy as they often add, remove, or amend coverages found on the standard policy.

**84. A:** The insuring agreement. The insuring agreement is the section of the insurance policy that states the insurance policy will provide services that may include payments to the insured for covered losses. The services and/or payments will only be provided by the insurance company if all the policy provisions are also followed by the insured. Such provisions may be timely notice of claim, securing the property from further damage, etc.

**85. C:** Salvage value. The salvage value is the numeric value given to a piece of property after it sustains damage. Marty's car, although inoperable, still holds value in that some of its parts can be used again.

**86. C:** HO-4. An HO-4 policy is a form of homeowners insurance that is designed to be purchased by the tenant of a location. This policy provides coverage for the tenant's personal property and does not provide coverage for the dwelling itself. Some landlords may require the tenant to purchase this type of policy prior to leasing their dwelling.

**87. D:** Liability. A commercial package policy combines property and liability coverage into one policy. Package policies are attractive to policyholders because they are often cheaper than purchasing two separate policies.

**88. B:** Business personal property. Business personal property includes property that is primarily housed in the building of the business and is used solely for the needs of the business. Some carriers may refer to this property as contents coverage. Business personal property includes furniture, fixtures, equipment, etc.

**89. A:** No, a company is required to obtain written consent prior to running a credit report. Under the Fair Credit Reporting Act, a company is required to obtain written consent prior to running a credit report. The company is not in compliance by checking Amber's credit without her written consent. Written consent is required regardless of the line of work except for the trucking industry.

**90. A:** Yes, but he will have to pay for it. An individual can request his credit score at any time from the credit bureau. The individual will have to pay to see the score in most cases. If the mortgage company is the one requesting the credit score, the mortgage company will not charge the individual.

**91. D:** Yes, you can dispute information that is inaccurate. Suzanna is allowed to dispute any inaccuracies on her own and does not need the mortgage company to do so on her behalf. The credit bureau must conduct an investigation on all disputes that are filed unless the dispute is obviously without merit.

**92. C:** 30 days. A credit bureau typically has to correct or remove any inaccuracies from an individual's credit report within 30 days. During the 30-day period before the error is corrected, the bureau can still report all accurate information.

**93. B:** The Gramm Leach Bliley Act. The Gramm Leach Bliley Act was designed around the need for insurance companies and banking companies to consolidate for the better good of the economy. This act enhanced competition in the banking and insurance industries and allowed for greater financial stability in the companies due to mergers. The act was signed in 1999 by President Clinton.

**94. B:** Claims-made. A claims-made policy is one in which the claim must be made during the policy period. Claims-made, however, has an extended reporting period which adds extra time in which the insured can report a claim. Hunter's policy would have to be set up as claims-made and in the extending reporting period in order to submit his claim.

**95. D:** Supplemental payments. Supplemental payments are meant to cover costs involved immediately after a claim, as in first aid, or costs involved in helping to defend against a claim, such as travel expenses. These supplementary payments are in addition to the policy limits for CGL and business auto policies.

**96. A:** Professional policy limits are often reduced by the supplemental payments. Most professional liability policies will pay for supplementary payments, but in term, these payments will reduce the limits available to the insured for the claim. Business auto and commercial general liability policies also will pay for approved supplementary payments, but these payments will not reduce the limits available for the policy.

**97. C:** Certificate of insurance. A certificate of insurance provides proof that the contractor has secured insurance. This certificate will provide the effective dates of the policy, as well as the limits available and what type of insurance policy it is. To ask for a certificate of insurance from a potential contract worker is common if there is a greater exposure to liability claims.

**98. A:** Proof of loss. The insured must provide proof of the loss in order for the insurance company to determine if the loss is covered. Proof may be photographs, video evidence, allowing the insurance company to view the damaged property, etc. It is important that the insured only take measures to prevent further loss to the property and not try to fix the property before the insurance company can view for evidence.

**99. C:** Concealment. Concealment is the act of not providing information or of withholding information which may be considered relevant to the insurance coverage. If an insured is found to have concealed information, the coverage may be voided by the insurance company.

**100. B:** Premises-operations. Premises-operations is a category of hazards resulting from damage by the insured's business operations while the operations are occurring on the Insured's premises. This type of exposure normally is covered by a general liability policy.

**101. D:** Away from the insured's premises. For products-completed operations coverage to apply, the loss must occur due to liability of the insured's product or operations while away from the insured's premises. The insured also must have completed the operations prior to the loss.

**102. B:** Ensuing fire. Ensuing fire is an exposure presented by earthquakes that is usually included on property policies as a covered exposure. Earthquake coverage itself is usually excluded on property policies but may be added by endorsement to some property policies.

**103. D:** An endorsed homeowners or stand-alone mobile home policy. Katherine can obtain an endorsed homeowners or a mobile home policy to cover the needs of her manufactured home. She will be able to have coverage that compares to a regular homeowners policy but that is tailored to the specialized needs of a mobile home or a manufactured home.

**104. A:** Yes, but the mortgagee in turn will take on all the responsibilities the insured previously held as owner of the policy. The mortgagee will be allowed continued coverage but must pay any premium due, notify insurer of changes in ownership, provide loss notification, etc. The mortgagee must in effect take on the conditions the policy sets for the policyholder.

**105. C:** Mortgagee clause. A mortgagee clause is a requirement by some financial institutions that provides protection in the event of a large loss or act of the insured which voids the policy. This clause is often required for larger home loans to individuals or loans for businesses for their office buildings.

**106. C:** No, it may be a specific dollar amount or a percentage of the property value. The wind and hail deductible can be expressed in many different ways. The deductible can be a specific dollar amount, a percentage of the policy limit, or a percentage of the property's value.

**107. D:** Homeowners, commercial property, and commercial liability coverage. A farmowners policy addresses the unique needs of farm operations for family operated farms. This type of policy incorporates the coverages afforded by homeowners, commercial property, and commercial liability insurance policies. Farmowners policies are not designed for larger risks or exposures presented by commercial farms.

**108. B:** Because farms have commercial as well as residential characteristics. Farms run by families or individuals are unique as opposed to large commercial or corporate farms. Farmowners policies cover this unique need by addressing the commercial and residential characteristics through the combination policy.

**109. A:** No, this is purchased through licensed insurance agents. Crop-hail insurance is not sold through federal government programs but rather is purchased through licensed agents. This coverage is sold with a premium based on past loss experience. The experience is not considered by individual experience but by the township or county as a whole.

**110. D:** Wind and fire. Wind and fire are two perils that may be added to crop-hail insurance. Wind and fire coverages are only available if the state allows them and may be specific to a certain type of crop. In areas of high wind exposure, the insured will likely pay a high premium to ensure proper coverage, if coverage is even available.

**111. B:** No, coverage will extend a specific number of days. In the event of a covered loss, repairs may be made but the office building may still not be fully functioning immediately after repairs are made. Business income coverage will extend a specified number of days after repairs are complete to allow the business to be fully up and running again.

**112. D:** Yes, with the insurer's consent. The process of transferring an insurance policy to another party is known as assignment. Assignment is only possible if the insurance company provides written consent to transfer the policy to the approved party.

**113. C:** To prevent or lessen the likelihood of lawsuits. Some professional insurance policies contain a waiver of subrogation to prevent lawsuits or claims from occurring. The cost of the insurance is spread among the parties to the contract, and once the claim is paid, the claim has ended.

**114. A:** Sources of underwriting information. Matt was requesting information needed to determine what type of coverage the policyholder needs and what type of coverage she would be eligible for. Sources of underwriting information may include an application, credit report, and motor vehicle report as well as an inspection of the property being covered.

**115. B:** Actual cash value. The actual cash value is the value given to a piece of property, such as an automobile, if there is a covered loss. Actual cash value is determined by the fair market value of the property or the cost to replace the property minus depreciation. Actual cash value is less desirable than replacement cost because it takes depreciation into account.

**116. A:** Fix the loss independently. The insured must not try to fix the loss before the insurer has a chance to survey the loss. The insured must, however, try to prevent the loss from becoming worse. An example would be if a roof leak occurred, the insured should tarp the roof to prevent further water damage. The insurer may also require the insured to send pictures of the loss or receipts for any repairs to the loss.

**117. D:** Slander. Bodily injury is a coverage addressed by most insurance policies. If covered, bodily injury includes physical injury to a party. This may include sickness, bodily harm, and even death as a result of injury. Disease is another aspect of bodily injury that may be covered.

**118. C:** No, it is added to claims-made policies at an additional cost. Tail coverage may be provided on claims-made policies, which allows a claim to be reported after the policy has expired. The loss must have occurred during the policy period, however, and an additional premium is due for the tail coverage provision.

**119. C:** No, because the claim was reported after the runoff period. Ryan's policy contains a five-year runoff period, which means the claim must be reported within five years of the policy ending. Another condition of the runoff period is that the loss must occur during the policy period.

**120. C:** The coverage triggers. Claims-made and occurrence are known as the coverage triggers for an insurance policy. Under the claims-made trigger, the claim must be reported during the policy period for coverage to apply. Under the occurrence trigger, the loss must occur during the policy period for coverage to apply.

# Practice Test #2

**1. Can a warranty be valid and enforced if not specifically written out in the contract?**
   a. No, a warranty must be written out in all cases
   b. Yes, a warranty written out is never a requirement
   c. Sometimes a warranty only need be expressed or implied
   d. No, warranties always must be written-out, signed contracts by both parties

**2. Howard was watching a TV commercial that advertised, "A household cleaner which could get rid of any type of grease stain." Howard purchased this product to remove a grease stain he had on his garage floor. After many attempts at cleaning using this product, the grease stain still remained. Could Howard file a claim against the cleaning company because its product did not work?**
   a. Yes, because express warranty exists
   b. Yes, because of negligence on behalf of the cleaning company
   c. No, because a written warranty does not exist
   d. No, because once a product leaves the manufacturer, no liability remains with the company that produced the product

**3. Name one way in which strict liability is different from negligence.**
   a. Under negligence claims, the nature or type of product is the issue
   b. Under strict liability, the nature or type of product is the issue for the claim
   c. Under strict liability, the claim is due to the direct actions of the party being sued
   d. Strict liability and negligence are one and the same

**4. Yolanda was injured while performing her daily duties at work. Under worker's compensation laws, will Yolanda have to prove her company was at fault for her injuries?**
   a. No, in the majority of cases, injury claims at work will be paid without proving fault
   b. Yes, worker's compensation laws always require that fault be proven
   c. Yes, unless there is a witness, you must always prove fault in an employment setting
   d. No, unless the employer demands that fault be proven, Yolanda will be compensated for her injuries

**5. Under which exception to the exclusive remedy approach are employees required to prove negligence on the part of their employer to receive compensation for an injury at work?**
   a. Employee liability
   b. No-fault employee laws
   c. Worker's exemption laws
   d. Employer's liability

**6. While employer's liability coverage does require fault to be proven by the employee, the coverage also has two advantages over workers' compensation coverage. Which two types of claims would be covered under employer's liability coverage but not workers' compensation coverage?**

   a. Third-party claims and loss of wages
   b. Dual capacity claims and third-party-over claims
   c. Dual capacity claims and bodily injury
   d. Third-party-over claims and bodily injury

**7. Under employer's liability coverage, can an employee sue an employer in addition to collecting through a workers' compensation claim?**

   a. Yes, in all cases
   b. No, in all cases
   c. Yes, under a dual capacity claim
   d. Yes, with no restrictions involved

**8. Lindsay suffered a loss to her property after a major storm hit her town. Lindsay wanted her homeowner's insurance to pay for the loss, but her insurance carrier wanted to deny the claim. The insurance carrier was looking to deny on the basis that Lindsay did not do enough to secure her property prior to the storm. If Lindsay and the insurance carrier cannot come to an agreement and wish to not proceed through the court system, what is another means they could use to determine fault?**

   a. Eyewitness
   b. They must proceed through the court system if an agreement cannot be reached
   c. Lindsay would win, because if there is a dispute between an insurance carrier and an insured, the insured always wins
   d. Arbitration

**9. Under which type of arbitration is the decision final?**

   a. Non-binding arbitration
   b. Non-discussion arbitration
   c. Absolute arbitration
   d. Binding arbitration

**10. Does non-binding arbitration always result in a final "winner"?**

   a. Yes, the "winner" is final in non-binding arbitration
   b. No, the non-winning party does not have to accept the arbitrator's decision
   c. Yes, the parties must leave the proceedings with a final winner or find a new arbitrator
   d. No, the "winner" must still win in a court of law

**11. Brent owned multiple properties, vehicles, and a couple of commercial locations. To cover all of Brent's exposures, he purchased a couple of different insurance policies. If Brent suffered a loss to one of his properties and more than one of his policies covered his loss, what could the insurance carriers do to determine which policy would pay?**

   a. Proceed with arbitration
   b. Determine which policy was issued first and that policy would pay
   c. Determine which policy had the highest limits and that policy would pay
   d. The loss would be automatically split among the policies

**12. All of the following are ways in which an insured can interfere with subrogation EXCEPT:**
   a. Interfere with the investigation
   b. Impair the investigation
   c. Provide the insurance carrier with complete documentation of the loss
   d. Withhold vital details about the loss

**13. When notifying the insurance carrier of a claim, does the insured have to submit the notice on a specific form or document?**
   a. Yes, a form specific to the insurance carrier must be completed
   b. No, a form, letter, or lawsuit could notify of a claim
   c. No, a simple call is always fine for reporting a claim
   d. Yes, anything other than a specific claim reporting form would be denied

**14. Michael was running late for a meeting at his job and did not lock his car door. When he realized it was unlocked, Michael did not want to turn around to go back and lock the vehicle. Michael thought if anything was stolen it was okay because his insurance would cover the loss. Which type of hazard has Michael committed by not going back to lock his car door?**
   a. Moral hazard
   b. Physical debris removal hazard
   c. Morale hazard
   d. Physical hazard

**15. Which type of insurance policy is designed to cover property in motion, regardless of the location?**
   a. Moveable risk policies
   b. Property in motion policies
   c. Transportation policies
   d. Inland marine policies

**16. Cole's house was destroyed by fire and was considered a total loss. Cole contacted his insurance company to assess the damage and hopefully receive a check to cover his damages. Cole was responsible for giving his insurance company a list of all damaged personal property lost from the fire. He knew his computer was in his car at the time of the fire and was not damaged, but Cole added the computer to the list to have the insurance company pay for a new one. Which hazard is Cole guilty of committing?**
   a. Moral hazard
   b. Ethical hazard
   c. Morale hazard
   d. Physical hazard

**17. Which type of coverage, afforded by some insurance policies, will cover all losses unless specifically noted as being an excluded loss?**
   a. Named perils
   b. All risks
   c. Excluded perils
   d. Excluded causes of loss

18. In addition to coverage for the building itself, commercial property coverage also covers all the losses below EXCEPT:
   a. Loss of income
   b. Increase in expenses
   c. Contents
   d. Commercial property coverage only covers loss to the building

19. Ralph owned a local convenience store that was damaged by a fire. The building suffered extensive damage and took several weeks to repair. Once the building was repaired, it still took Ralph a few days to get his store up and running again. Assuming this loss was covered by insurance, which specific coverage would extend to pay the loss suffered during the couple days after the repairs were complete but the store was still not 100 percent open?
   a. Commercial property coverage
   b. Commercial extension coverage
   c. Business income coverage
   d. Business extension coverage

20. The roof on Randy's T-shirt store collapsed following a heavy snowstorm. A lot of Randy's inventory was damaged, but he was able to salvage some merchandise. While his store was being repaired, Randy rented a storage unit in which to store his saved merchandise until the store was ready. This extra expense may be paid by which coverage part of commercial property insurance?
   a. Extra expense coverage
   b. Unforeseen expense coverage
   c. Business exception coverage
   d. Business additional income coverage

21. Actual cash value is determined by subtracting which value from the replacement cost value of a specific piece of property?
   a. Depreciation value
   b. Actual replacement value
   c. Wear and tear value
   d. Actual value plus

22. Replacement cost is a form of loss valuation in which the insured's property is replaced by which method?
   a. Market value
   b. Cost to replace property with property of the same or equal value
   c. Actual cash value
   d. Salvage value

23. Christine was moving to a new town for a job change and decided to rent a townhouse. Which type of homeowners policy should Christine purchase to protect her exposures as a tenant?
   a. HO-2
   b. HO-3
   c. HO-8
   d. HO-4

**24. The HO-5 type of homeowners policy provides coverage on an all-risks basis for all exposures EXCEPT:**
   a. Personal property
   b. Dwelling
   c. Tenant's personal vehicle
   d. Other structures

**25. Broad and basic forms both provide coverage on various homeowners policies. Which form, broad or basic, provides the most coverage against losses?**
   a. Broad form
   b. Basic form
   c. Both have equal amounts of perils insured against
   d. It depends on the type of policy

**26. Which type of homeowners policy is designed for homeowners who own a house on the town's historic registry?**
   a. HO-2
   b. HO-3
   c. HO-4
   d. HO-8

**27. Which type of homeowners policy provides coverage for the dwelling on a broad form?**
   a. HO-2
   b. HO-5
   c. HO-6
   d. HO-8

**28. Courtney was driving to an interview for a new job. She was running late and saw that the light had just turned red. Courtney proceeded through the red light because she did not want to waste time sitting at the traffic light, and she did not fully check to see if any other cars were around. A car, however, was driving through the intersection after seeing the light turn green, and this car and Courtney's collided. Courtney would be cited as the party at fault due to her being what?**
   a. Speeding
   b. Negligent
   c. Not paying attention to the scene around her
   d. Courtney would not be cited

**29. A personal articles floater can be a stand-alone policy or an endorsement to a homeowners policy to provide coverage for all the following exposures EXCEPT:**
   a. Fine arts
   b. Stamps
   c. Fixtures
   d. Jewelry

30. Harry was involved in an accident in which a deer ran out in front of him in the road and into the front of Harry's vehicle. Harry's insurance included other-than-collision coverage subject to him paying the first $250 of any loss sustained. Harry's $250 payment requirement is known as which term in insurance?

   a. First-party payment
   b. Deductible
   c. Retention
   d. Policy premium

31. A commercial property floater is coverage designed for commercial exposures that do not remain at a fixed location. For which type of commercial exposure would you potentially purchase a commercial property floater?

   a. An office printer
   b. An auto gifted to an employee as part of her benefits package
   c. A food cart that travels to a different location each week
   d. Office fixtures

32. Erin is a renewal underwriter for ABC Insurance. She was reviewing an umbrella policy for an operator who just turned 90 years of age. According to ABC's guidelines, an insured is only eligible for limits up to $1 million if he or she is over the age of 89. Erin's insured currently has limits of $2 million. What will Erin need to issue to notify the insured that his coverage is being restricted if she binds the renewal quote?

   a. Nonrenewal notice
   b. Notice of limits change
   c. Notice of guideline change
   d. Conditional renewal

33. Jen was a renewal underwriter for ABC Insurance. Jen was reviewing a claim that just came into ABC for an Insured she has serviced for five years. The claim's severity exceeded ABC's guidelines of reserve amounts and Jen was required by this guideline to stop writing this risk. What type of notice is Jen required to send to the insured to advise him that coverage would not be renewed?

   a. Nonrenewal notice
   b. Conditional renewal
   c. Cancellation notice
   d. Notice of excess loss

34. Frank was an underwriter in the personal lines department. He received an application for a personal umbrella, which had all the required information, but the application was not signed. According to Frank's department guidelines, he could provide a temporary notice of coverage but could not fully issue the policy until the application was signed by the insured. What is this temporary notice of coverage known as?

   a. An endorsement
   b. A pre-policy form
   c. A short-form policy
   d. A binder

35. Tiffany has an insurance policy through ABC Insurance. Tiffany notified her carrier that she was moving from New Jersey to Florida and would like her policy to reflect this change. ABC was not licensed to write business in Florida and informed Tiffany that it would need to cancel her policy. What method would ABC use to cancel Tiffany's policy and return any unearned premium?

   a. Short rate method
   b. Pro rata method
   c. It would not be allowed to cancel and would have to continue to write her policy
   d. Mid-term method

36. Andrea has her insurance policy through her local agent. Andrea's friend opened his own insurance agency and promised Andrea lower rates if she switched her policy to his office. When Andrea informed her current agent that she wanted her coverage cancelled, which method of cancellation will he use?

   a. Short rate method
   b. Pro rata method
   c. He would not be allowed to cancel and would have to continue to write her policy
   d. Mid-term method

37. Griffin decided to spend the night camping with friends in a wildlife reserve. This area prohibited camping because it was known to house a large brown bear population. Griffin and his friends knew of the bear risk but still spent the night there. In the morning, Griffin woke up to a brown bear eating their food. When he tried to scare the bear away, the bear turned to attack Griffin. He suffered multiple cuts before his friends were able to scare the bear away from him. Would Griffin be allowed to sue the township for his injuries due to them happening inside the reserve?

   a. Yes, due to the location, the township would be responsible
   b. Yes, a park ranger should have secured the scene better for campers
   c. No, strict liability would apply due to Griffin knowing the risks and still camping out
   d. No, the reserve does not have to protect in any situation

38. The Peterson family has an insurance policy through ABC Insurance. During the middle of their policy term, the Petersons purchased an additional vehicle and wanted this vehicle added to their insurance policy. What would ABC Insurance process to show an additional vehicle on their policy?

   a. Issue a binder
   b. Issue an entire new policy
   c. Issue an endorsement
   d. Nothing, they would always just change at renewal

39. Curtis was a 10-year-old who played on his township's baseball team. While at practice one day, Curtis was playing catch with a teammate when his ball struck a car windshield. The windshield was shattered and glass injured the person inside. This person sued Curtis' coach for her injuries and property damage. Could Curtis' coach be liable for this claim?

   a. No, the coach had no control over where Curtis was playing catch
   b. Yes, if she can prove vicarious liability
   c. Yes, a child cannot be responsible for his actions
   d. No, Curtis is the only party who could be sued

40. Which organization is responsible for developing many of the standard policy forms and endorsements that make up an insurance policy?

   a. FEMA
   b. Insurance Exchange
   c. Insurance Management Department
   d. Insurance Services Office Inc.

41. In insurance, different policies are issued to protect against specific causes of loss. What is the term used to describe a cause of loss?

   a. Peril
   b. Exposure
   c. Loss cause
   d. Loss potential

42. Jason was in the market for a new car. His current car was starting to have repair issues, but it was still very much a useable vehicle. When Jason goes to trade in his car, which value does the dealership use to determine a starting point for how much his car is worth?

   a. Replacement value
   b. Market value
   c. Salvage value
   d. Dealership value

43. Michael went out with a group of his guy friends for a night at the casinos. He planned on gambling most of the night in hopes to win money. Which type of risk is Michael involved in by gambling?

   a. Speculative risk
   b. Pure risk
   c. True risk
   d. Definite risk

44. Kelsey was booking a flight to visit her family in New York. Whenever a person travels, she runs the risk of a loss due to the nature of travel. Which type of risk is Kelsey involved in by traveling in an airplane?

   a. Speculative risk
   b. Pure risk
   c. True risk
   d. Definite risk

45. Which type of government-funded insurance program will respond to direct damage from natural disasters, such as floods, to a building?

   a. Natural disaster relief
   b. Natural flood relief
   c. National Flood Insurance Program
   d. National Disaster Program

**46. Which cause of loss form provides coverage for property damage due to falling objects?**
   a. Basic
   b. Simple
   c. All causes of loss
   d. Broad

**47. All of the following perils are insured against under the Basic Cause of Loss Form EXCEPT:**
   a. Vandalism
   b. Riot
   c. Weight of sleet
   d. Smoke

**48. Which cause of loss form will specifically list any and all perils the policy will provide coverage for?**
   a. Basic
   b. Broad
   c. Open perils
   d. Named perils

**49. Which cause of loss form will specifically list any perils the policy will not insure against?**
   a. Basic
   b. Broad
   c. Open perils
   d. Named perils

**50. Which endorsement that may be added to a policy would suspend coverage if a building stood vacant over a specific period of time?**
   a. Vacancy permit endorsement
   b. Occupancy permit endorsement
   c. Vacant coverage form
   d. Occupancy extension endorsement

**51. Statutes of limitations are placed on claims for a variety of reasons, and the length of the statute depends on the specific claim. What is the statute of limitation for filing a medical malpractice claim?**
   a. Three years
   b. The statute is state specific
   c. Five years
   d. Ten years

**52. Under a D&O policy, are defense cost covered within the policy limits?**
   a. No, defense costs are in excess of the limits
   b. Yes, defense costs are included in the limits
   c. Yes, but only if the insured pays an extra premium
   d. No, defense costs are never covered by a D&O policy

**53. Which type of insurance policy does not provide coverage for bodily injury and property damage?**

   a. Homeowners
   b. Auto
   c. D&O
   d. Commercial package

**54. Gerry was driving to work one day when his car was hit by a driver who ran a red light. The driver who hit Gerry did not have auto insurance and Gerry was concerned over who would pay for the damage to his car. Gerry's agent told him his own insurance would cover the cost due to which coverage included in Gerry's policy?**

   a. Underinsured motorist coverage
   b. Non-insurance coverage
   c. Other motorist coverage
   d. Uninsured motorist coverage

**55. Kelly was driving home from vacation when she was rear ended at a stop sign. The driver who hit Kelly had auto insurance, but at a very low limit. The limit the driver had would not cover the extent of the damage to Kelly's vehicle. Which coverage, if Kelly had it on her own policy, would cover the difference between what the damage cost and what the at-fault driver's limits were?**

   a. Underinsured motorist coverage
   b. Uninsured motorist coverage
   c. Other motorist coverage
   d. Non-insurance coverage

**56. The split limits approach is one way in which an insurance policy will show the limits of coverage available for that specific policy. If a policy is written with split limits, what does the first limit indicate?**

   a. The maximum amount paid to a single person
   b. The maximum amount paid for all injured parties
   c. The maximum amount paid for property damage
   d. The minimum amount paid for property damage

**57. What is covered under the second limit indicated in the split limits approach?**

   a. The maximum amount paid to a single person
   b. The maximum amount paid for all injured parties
   c. The maximum amount paid for property damage
   d. The minimum amount paid to a single person

**58. Andy was driving to work one day when he became distracted and hit another vehicle. Andy's insurance policy follows the split limit approach. Which limit would Andy's insurance policy use to determine the amount of coverage available for the property damage to the vehicle Andy hit?**

   a. Limit one
   b. Property damage is excluded under the split limits approach
   c. Limit two
   d. Limit three

**59.** Greg was involved in a car accident with another vehicle in which Greg was found to be at fault. Which coverage under his auto insurance would pay for damage to the other vehicle?

a. Accident coverage
b. Other-than-collision coverage
c. Collision coverage
d. Accidental damage coverage

**60.** An insurance policy will typically display the limit or limits available in one of two ways. Split limits is the approach to showing different limits to respond to bodily injury and property damage. Which approach shows only one limit to cover any loss, whether it is bodily injury or property damage?

a. Split limit
b. Combined single limit
c. Per occurrence limit
d. Per person limit

**61.** Hillary was driving home from work one day when she rear ended another vehicle. The other driver was injured and needed medical attention. Which limit, under the Hillary's split limits policy, would respond to cover the medical cost?

a. Limit one
b. Limit two
c. Limit three
d. Limit four

**62.** Which type of automobile coverage would apply if an accident occurred and the insured needed to rent a vehicle for a temporary period of time?

a. Hired auto coverage
b. Rental assistance coverage
c. Rental reimbursement coverage
d. Rented auto coverage

**63.** If an insured wishes to rent a vehicle while traveling, would she need to purchase special insurance in order to drive a rental car?

a. Yes, in all cases
b. Yes, but the insured would be reimbursed by their primary auto carrier
c. Yes, but she can be reimbursed if no accident occurs
d. No, the rental car would have coverage under the insured's primary auto policy

**64.** Rex was severely injured in an auto accident. Rex was not at fault and was in the process of suing the other party for damages. Included in the damages, Rex was asking for damages to be paid towards his pain and suffering. Under which type of damages are pain and suffering included?

a. General damages
b. Special damages
c. Pain and suffering damages
d. Bodily injury damages

65. Galen was severely injured in an auto accident in which she was not at fault. Galen required extensive medical care, including months of therapy, to recover from her injuries. If Galen were to sue, which type of damages would she sue for her medical costs?

   a. General damages
   b. Special damages
   c. Pain and suffering damages
   d. Bodily injury damages

66. Auto and trailer dealers should purchase which type of policy to cover their liability exposures?

   a. Auto and trailers insurance
   b. Garage keepers coverage
   c. Bailer coverage
   d. Bailee coverage

67. Under a garage keepers policy, liability on which party must be determined in order for coverage to apply?

   a. The car owner
   b. The employee
   c. The insured
   d. The manufacturer of the vehicle

68. Under garage keepers extra legal liability coverage, does liability need to be determined for coverage to apply?

   a. No, liability only needs to be determined if the court asks
   b. Yes, liability must be determined in all cases for coverage to apply
   c. No, liability does not need to be determined for coverage to apply
   d. Yes, liability must be determined or coverage will be limited

69. If it can be proven that there was willful negligence on the part of an employer, are employees barred from filing a tort claim due to an injury?

   a. Yes, the employees are still barred
   b. Yes, for all cases
   c. No, willful negligence does not need to be proved unless ordered by a court
   d. No, if the employer also does not obtain proper insurance coverage

70. Under a DP (dwelling package policy), does the insured location have to be occupied by the owner of the property?

   a. Yes, in all cases
   b. Yes, the owner needs to occupy 50 percent of the property
   c. No, the property can be tenant occupied
   d. No, the tenant must occupy 50 percent of the property

71. The DP-3 special form offers coverage for dwellings on an all-risks basis, but offers coverage to personal property under which cause of loss form?

   a. Broad named perils
   b. Basic named perils
   c. All risks
   d. Coverage for personal property is excluded under a DP-3

72. A DP-1 policy provides coverage for the dwelling according to which cause of loss form?
   a. Broad form
   b. All risks
   c. DP-1 excludes coverage for the dwelling itself
   d. Basic form

73. Which dwelling package form of insurance provides coverage for the dwelling on a broad form?
   a. DP-1
   b. DP-2
   c. DP-3
   d. DP-8

74. An insurance policy is made up of several parts. Which part acts as the agreement or contract between the insurance company and the policyholder?
   a. Declarations
   b. Insuring agreement
   c. Conditions
   d. Policy jacket

75. Loss of income coverage is insurance that provides for loss of income due to the interruption of business caused by a covered loss. For how long does loss of income coverage typically apply?
   a. 30 days
   b. 60 days
   c. 90 days
   d. 120 days

76. Greg and Janelle Smith were shopping around for an auto insurance plan for their household. After meeting with several agents, they realized that a DUI on Greg's driving record was making the quotes on their premiums drastically higher than they expected. Greg and Janelle were meeting with their last agent to discuss prices and the agent failed to run their MVR. Greg and Janelle purchased their auto policy from this agent, secretly hoping the agent would not ask about the driving record. Greg and Janelle are guilty of what by hiding Greg's DUI charge?
   a. Lying
   b. Forgery
   c. Concealment
   d. Perjury

77. Exclusive remedy prohibits an employee from filing what type of claim against his employers?
   a. Tort liability
   b. Workers compensation
   c. Employer's negligence
   d. Punitive damages

78. Products-completed operations is coverage provided on a general liability policy. Where must the injury occur for products-completed operations liability to apply?

   a. At the insured's premises
   b. Within 10 miles of the insured's premises
   c. Away from the insured's premises
   d. At or away from the insured's premises

79. Libel, copyright infringement and slander are some of the offenses that are covered under what type of general liability coverage?

   a. Marketing injury
   b. Written injury
   c. Emotional injury
   d. Advertising injury

80. Dwelling package policies provide coverage for numerous types of exposures. Are the exposures associated with farming covered adequately by a DP policy?

   a. Yes, the DP-1 covers farms
   b. No, farms are excluded under all dwelling package forms
   c. Yes, the DP-2 covers farms
   d. Yes, the DP-3 covers farms

81. Which act requires notification to the insured, as well as an option to opt out, before providing the insured's personal information to a third party?

   a. Gramm-Leach-Bliley
   b. Bliley-Creed
   c. Third Party Coverage
   d. Consumer Protection Doctrine

82. A car, a box of records, jewelry, and expensive clothing are all which type of property?

   a. Intangible property
   b. Tangible property
   c. Business exposures
   d. Commercial personal property

83. Frances was in the market for a secondary home at the beach. She saved up for years to purchase this house and when she was finally ready, Frances made an offer on a home. Before the sale can be completed, the mortgage company writing her home loan will need to run a credit check on Frances. Will Frances be responsible for paying for the credit check or will the seller of the home be responsible?

   a. Frances will be responsible
   b. The seller will be responsible
   c. Frances and the seller will split the cost of the credit check
   d. The mortgage company handles the cost of the credit check

84. Stocks, bonds, mutual fund investments, patents, etc., are which type of property?

   a. Intangible property
   b. Tangible property
   c. Financial property
   d. Business personal property

85. Erin was planning on purchasing her first home in the next two years. She was researching which areas she would like to buy in as well as how much money she would need saved for a down payment. Erin's realtor told her to make sure her credit was excellent to get the best rate possible for her mortgage. If Erin wanted to check her credit score now, who would be responsible for the cost?

   a. Erin's realtor
   b. Erin cannot request a credit score without a signed agreement of sale
   c. Erin
   d. Credit scores are always free

86. When Erin received her credit score, she noticed some errors on her report. There were a couple of delinquent charges listed on her report from a couple years ago that Erin knew were false. Is Erin allowed to file a dispute to fight the discrepancies on her report?

   a. No, you can never dispute a credit report
   b. Yes, in all cases
   c. No, only a bank can dispute for you
   d. Yes, if the dispute is with merit

87. Supplemental payments are often needed immediately following a loss. Are supplemental payments in addition to the policy limits for CGL and business auto policies, or are the payments included in the limits available?

   a. Included in
   b. Supplemental payments are not offered under CGL but are under business auto policies
   c. In addition to
   d. Supplemental payments are not offered under business auto policies but are under CGL policies

88. Beatrice owned a mobile home as a secondary property in a mountain resort campsite. Would Beatrice need to secure a stand-alone policy to cover her needs for this home or would an endorsement to her homeowners be sufficient?

   a. It would depend on the carrier; some will write with an endorsement, while others offer a stand-alone policy
   b. She would only be able to obtain a stand-alone policy
   c. She would only be able to obtain coverage through an endorsement to her homeowners policy
   d. There is no coverage available for mobile homes through independent agencies

89. ABC Farms is a large, commercial farm that generates $10 million in revenue each year. ABC's operations include raising cows and pigs for later sale of their meat to local restaurants, a commercial store open to the public daily, as well as seasonal events. Would ABC Farms be eligible for farmowners insurance?

   a. Yes, it fits the requirements for farmowners insurance
   b. No, farmowners is for family-operated farms with minimal commercial exposure
   c. No, ABC does not generate enough revenue to qualify for farmowners insurance
   d. Yes, due to the sale of meat to local restaurants and not worldwide sales

**90. Is liability a covered exposure under a commercial package policy?**

a. No, liability is never included
b. Yes, liability and auto coverage
c. Yes, liability and errors and omissions coverage
d. Yes, liability and property coverage

**91. Darrell's home suffered a fire loss in which most of his possessions were damaged. If Darrell's insurance carrier is requesting a list of all damaged property and its worth, what might the carrier demand if the worth of property is questionable?**

a. A third-party opinion
b. A signed statement from Darrell
c. An appraisal
d. The carrier cannot question the worth of property damaged by a covered loss

**92. Elle's insurance policy is a claims-made policy written with effective dates of January 1, 2013 – January 1, 2014. Her policy also states that any claim that occurs before January 1, 2013, is excluded regardless of the claim being reported during the policy period. What is January 1, 2013, known as in this case?**

a. The claims-made date
b. The retroactive date
c. The claims reporting start date
d. The claims-made reporting date

**93. What is one of the primary coverages provided by a commercial crime policy?**

a. Employee misrepresentation
b. Bodily injury
c. Employee dishonesty
d. Workers compensation

**94. What does a surety bond guarantee?**

a. A claim will be paid in full
b. An inspection will be performed
c. Another party will fulfill its promise
d. Another party will be responsible for any and all payments

**95. A surety bond consists of three separate parties. Which party is responsible for carrying out the work or performance stated in the contract?**

a. The surety
b. The obligee
c. The policyholder
d. The principal

**96. Of the three parties that make up a surety bond, which party is the one that is on the receiving end of the promise made or the contract signed?**

a. The obligee
b. The surety
c. The policyholder
d. The principal

97. Which party in the surety bond contract is the party that is guaranteeing the work or performance of a second party?
   a. The obligee
   b. The surety
   c. The policyholder
   d. The principal

98. Which type of insurance carrier is required under the Terrorism Risk Insurance Act (TRIS) of 2002 to write policies that will protect again acts of terrorism?
   a. Commercial insurers
   b. Personal lines insurers
   c. Niche market insurers
   d. Auto insurers

99. Errors and omissions (E&O) insurance, which is a policy common in professional lines of insurance, was formed to primarily cover what types of losses?
   a. Bodily injury
   b. Property damage
   c. Libel
   d. Financial losses

100. All of the following are exclusions under a medical malpractice insurance policy EXCEPT:
   a. Punitive damages
   b. Sexual misconduct
   c. Non-intentional acts
   d. Criminal acts

101. Is a medical malpractice insurance policy written on a claims-made or on an occurrence basis?
   a. Could be either claims-made or occurrence
   b. Claims-made
   c. Occurrence
   d. Depends on the type of claim

102. A directors and officers (D&O) liability insurance policy is designed to protect all of the following parties EXCEPT:
   a. Director of a non-profit
   b. Manager of a for-profit company
   c. Officer of a privately held firm
   d. Director of an educational institution

103. Are director and officers (D&O) liability policies written on a claims-made or an occurrence basis?
   a. A D&O policy can be written either way
   b. Occurrence basis
   c. Claims-made
   d. There is no specific coverage trigger on D&O policies

**104. Under a commercial general liability policy, are defense costs included in the limits or in addition to the limits available on the policy?**

　　a. Defense costs are in addition to the policy limits
　　b. They are included in the limits
　　c. Depends on the specific policy
　　d. Defense costs are not covered by a commercial general liability policy

**105. Are bodily injury and property damages claims covered under a director & officers policy?**

　　a. Yes, in all cases
　　b. Bodily injury is covered, but not property damage
　　c. Property damage is, but not bodily injury
　　d. No, both bodily injury and property damage claims are not covered under a D&O policy

**106. All of the following are advantages to purchasing a stand-alone versus a packaged employment practices policy EXCEPT:**

　　a. Higher premium costs
　　b. Option to select "duty to defend" or "non-duty to defend"
　　c. Broader scope of coverage under the stand-alone
　　d. Risk management services available under a stand-alone policy

**107. What is a disadvantage to writing a stand-alone employment practices liability policy?**

　　a. Lower costs than a package policy
　　b. Risk management
　　c. Broader scope of coverages
　　d. Having another policy to pay for and service

**108. While earthquake coverage is typically excluded under most policies, which peril associated with earthquakes is covered?**

　　a. Explosion
　　b. Ensuing fire
　　c. Property damage
　　d. Vehicle damage

**109. Commercial property policies attempt to address all common exposures from which an insured may face a loss. If an insured wishes to purchase additional coverage for exposures not included in a commercial property policy, what type of policy might the insured purchase?**

　　a. A second commercial property policy
　　b. An E&O policy
　　c. A direct response policy
　　d. A difference-in-conditions policy

**110. How is crop-hail insurance typically rated?**

　　a. The federal government sets the rates
　　b. Township or county rated
　　c. Insurance companies determine their individual rates
　　d. The state department determines the rates

**111. Wind and fire coverage can be added as additional covered perils to what type of insurance policy?**
    a. Crop-hail insurance
    b. Auto insurance
    c. Commercial property insurance
    d. Earthquake insurance

**112. Builder's risk policies provide coverage for all of the following during the course of construction EXCEPT:**
    a. Building materials
    b. Construction workers' personal auto
    c. Fixtures being used to build
    d. Equipment used in building the structure

**113. When should a builder's risk policy be obtained?**
    a. After the project begins
    b. Once the builder can walk on the site
    c. Once money is received for the project
    d. Before the project begins

**114. The portion of premium that is returned to the insured after the cancellation of a policy is known as what?**
    a. Cancellation premium
    b. Earned premium
    c. Return premium
    d. Unearned premium

**115. In order to obtain an insurance policy, Julie's agent was requesting several pieces of information to underwrite her risk. All of the following are common pieces of underwriting documents needed to write a risk EXCEPT:**
    a. 10-year look back on driving record
    b. Application
    c. Motor vehicle report
    d. Name and age of all vehicle operators in the household

**116. If a policy is written with an occurrence trigger, when does the loss have to occur for coverage to apply?**
    a. After the retroactive date
    b. It does not matter when the loss occurs, the claim just needs to be made during the policy period
    c. During the policy period
    d. Before the policy period

**117. What are the two coverage triggers common to commercial insurance policies?**
    a. Occurrence and first exposure
    b. Claims-made and occurrence
    c. Claims-made and proximate cause of loss
    d. First exposure and first response to loss

**118. When a policy is written with a claims-made trigger, when does the claim have to be made in order for coverage to apply?**

   a. Before the retroactive date
   b. After the retroactive date and with no end date requirement
   c. During the policy period
   d. Both the loss and claim reporting must occur during the policy period

**119. When a loss occurs, sometimes there is more than one event or exposure that caused the loss. What is known as the cause, or exposure, that most directly led to the loss?**

   a. Proximate cause
   b. Initial cause
   c. First cause
   d. Primary cause

**120. Does the insurance carrier have any duties after a policy is written but the policy period is still in effect?**

   a. No, once the policy is written, the carrier has fulfilled its duties
   b. Yes, but only if a claim arises
   c. Yes, for claims or to notify the insured of any changes that may affect his policy
   d. No, unless the insured requests the insurance carrier to perform a task

# Answer Key and Explanations

**1. C:** Sometimes a warranty only need be expressed or implied. In order for a warranty to be valid or enforced, the warranty must be written out, expressed or implied depending on the situation. A warranty is a contractual agreement that guarantees the performance or completion of a specific sale.

**2. A:** Yes, because express warranty exists. Howard purchased the cleaning product because the company expressed a promise that the cleaning solution would get rid of any type of grease stain. An express warranty may allow an individual to file a claim when they could otherwise not file based on negligence.

**3. B:** Under strict liability, the nature or type of product is the issue for the claim. To file a strict liability claim, the issue lies in whether the product was designed or manufactured in a way that would make the product harmful to the purchaser. Strict liability claims do not focus on whether or not negligence on the part of the defendant was present.

**4. A:** No, the majority of times injury claims at work will be paid without proving fault. Under workers' compensation laws, an employee will not have to prove where fault lies when injured at work in nearly every situation. These claims are also paid without court system involvement in the majority of cases.

**5. D:** Employer's liability. Under employer's liability coverage, the employee is required to prove negligence on the part of his or her employer to receive compensation for an injury at work. This is an exception to the norm for workers' compensation, which usually does not require fault to be proven. Employer's liability coverage is used in cases where employees are not covered by workers' compensation laws.

**6. B:** Dual capacity claims and third-party-over claims. Dual capacity claims and third-party-over claims are both eligible claims for coverage under employer's liability coverage but not under workers compensation. Third-party-over coverage applies when an employee sues a third party for her injuries. Dual capacity claims involve an injured employee who sues his employer through a product liability suit in addition to a workers' compensation claim.

**7. C:** Yes, under a dual capacity claim. Dual capacity claims are one of two claims covered under employer's liability coverage. Dual capacity claims allow the employee to sue her employer for her sustained injury in addition to pursuing coverage through workers' compensation benefits. The employee would be suing the employer in a product liability claim and not solely for being her employer and being injured at work.

**8. D:** Arbitration. Arbitration is a process used when two parties cannot come to an agreement. Arbitration consists of a third party who reviews all the facts and rules in favor of one party. The arbitrator is a neutral party decided on by both parties.

**9. D:** Binding arbitration. Under binding arbitration, both parties must follow the arbitrator's decision. This type of arbitration is required by some states in order for the claim to settle.

**10. B:** No, the non-winning party does not have to accept the arbitrator's decision. Under non-binding arbitration, the "winner" is not final, as both parties have the right to not accept the arbitrator's ruling. The "winner," though, will have leverage to bring to future arbitrator's or court appearances as having "won" once before.

**11. A:** Proceed with arbitration. Arbitration is not solely used to settle disputes between an insurer and an insurance company. Arbitration can be used when more than one insurance policy is in force and each policy covers the loss in question. The arbitrator will determine which policy will respond to the loss and for what amount.

**12. C:** Provide the insurance carrier with complete documentation of the loss. Part of the insured's duties after a loss is to assist the insurance carrier with any documentation or proof of loss it may need. The insured, however, may not interfere with the subrogation process itself or could face being responsible for the amount the carrier could have collected from the negligent party.

**13. B:** No, a form, letter, or lawsuit could notify of a claim. The claim process can be started by the insured submitting a loss notice ACCORD form, letter, or lawsuit notification. Each will prompt the insurance carrier to start a claims file and then begin the claims investigation process.

**14. C:** Morale hazard. Michael has created a morale hazard by knowing his vehicle was unlocked and refusing to lock the doors to prevent a theft. Michael is relying on his insurance carrier to cover any loss to his vehicle or personal property inside the vehicle.

**15. D:** Inland marine policies. An inland marine policy is a type of insurance policy that is designed to cover property in motion, regardless of the location. Inland marine policies can cover moveable property as well as property used for transportation – bridges, piers, etc.

**16. A:** Moral hazard. Cole committed a moral hazard by lying to his insurance company to receive money for a new computer. Cole knew his actions were wrong, but lied to profit from his fire loss. A moral hazard, if caught, could lead to the insurance company completely denying a claim or paying much less than the full amount of the claim.

**17. B:** All risks. All risks, or "open peril," coverage will provide cover for all losses unless specifically noted as being an excluded loss. This type of coverage affords the insured the broadest scope of coverage, as it allows for more covered perils than other coverage types.

**18. D:** Commercial property coverage only covers loss to the building. Commercial property coverage provides coverage not only for the building itself, but also for the contents, an increase in expenses due to the loss, and loss of income. This type of coverage is designed to protect businesses from not just a physical loss but also loss sustained while they try to rebuild.

**19. C:** Business income coverage. Business income coverage is part of commercial property insurance that provides coverage for income loss due to damage to the business' property. This coverage may be extended if after the repairs are complete, the business still requires a couple days before it can be running again.

**20. A:** Extra expense coverage. Extra expense coverage may be part of a business' commercial property insurance. This coverage provides for expenses that are outside of the normal scope of business expenses. Randy, under normal circumstances, would not have needed a storage unit, but due to damage from a covered loss, the storage unit became a necessary expense.

**21. A:** Depreciation value. Actual cash value is determined by subtracting the depreciation value from the replacement cost value of a specific piece of property. Actual cash value is less desirable for the insured than replacement cost coverage because the value paid is lower.

**22. B:** Cost to replace property with property of the same or equal value. Replacement cost is ideal for an insured, as it will replace his property with property of similar or equal value. Replacement cost does not take into account depreciation or wear and tear.

**23. D:** HO-4. An HO-4 policy is designed to meet the unique needs of tenants. This type of policy does not provide protection for the dwelling itself but rather the contents or personal property of the tenant. The HO-4 is not for owner-occupants due to the coverage not extending to the building itself.

**24. C:** Tenant's personal vehicles. The HO-5 type of a homeowners policy provides coverage on an all-risks basis for personal property, dwelling, and other structures. This product is designed for owner-occupants and not for providing coverage specifically for the tenant. The HO-5 provides the broadest coverage for homeowners.

**25. A:** Broad form. Broad form of loss adds additional perils to those already provided by the basic form. Such additional perils include collapse, falling objects, and weight from snow. Perils covered by basic and broad include hail, fire, and riot.

**26. D:** HO-8. The HO-8 modified homeowners form is a homeowners product designed for the unique needs of houses on the historic registry or other types of unique homes, whose replacement cost is higher than the market value. This policy provides coverage on the basic form.

**27. A:** HO-2. An HO-2 policy form provides, on a broad form of loss, coverage for the dwelling and other structures. Medical payments and personal liability are also coverages provided under the HO-2 homeowners policy form.

**28. B:** Negligent. Courtney was acting in a negligent manner when she drove through the red light. Courtney did not act as a prudent person would when driving according to traffic laws, and due to her negligence, she caused an accident.

**29. C:** Fixtures. A personal articles floater can be a stand-alone policy or an endorsement to a homeowners to provide coverage for fine arts, silverware, jewelry, and stamps. These types of exposures may have unique attributes or require higher coverage amounts than a homeowners policy without the personal articles floater endorsement could provide.

**30. B:** Deductible. The deductible is the portion of the loss payment for which the insured is responsible. The deductible must be met before the insurance carrier will submit its share in the rest of the loss payment. The deductible's intent is to put some responsibility on the insured for losses sustained.

**31. C:** A cart used to sell food that travels to a different location each week. A commercial property floater is a type of coverage endorsed onto a property insurance policy. This coverage is designed for commercial exposures that are not kept at a fixed location but instead travel from location to location.

**32. D:** Conditional renewal. Erin would need to issue a conditional renewal to notify the insured that he is being restricted in the amount of coverage he can purchase this term. A conditional renewal notice is often a requirement of the state and must be sent within the time frame outlined in the state's guidelines.

**33. A:** Nonrenewal notice. Jen would be required to send formal notice to the insured that his coverage would not be renewed in the form of a nonrenewal notice. Each state has set guidelines for reasons that you are able to non-renew and a time frame in which you can send the nonrenewal.

**34. D:** A binder. Frank could issue a binder for his insured until the application was signed. A binder is a temporary form notifying coverage is in place. A policy must still be fully issued, but the binder can serve as temporary proof of insurance coverage.

**35. B:** Pro rata method. ABC Insurance would use the pro rata method of cancellation to cancel Tiffany's policy. It is ABC's decision or guideline to cancel this policy so Tiffany should not be penalized. ABC would return the unearned premium to Tiffany without applying a short rate penalty deducted from the amount due.

**36. A:** Short rate method. Andrea would be penalized for cancelling her policy prior to the expiration date. Andrea's carrier would apply the short rate method against the unearned premium from the policy. The penalty is intended to discourage insured parties from cancelling their policies midterm to write with another carrier.

**37. C:** No, strict liability would apply due to Griffin knowing the risks and still camping out. Strict liability would apply because there was an inherent, known risk of the brown bears, and Griffin and his friends still camped in the reserve. The township is not liable, as it prohibits camping due to the risks involved.

**38. C:** Issue an endorsement. An endorsement is an amendment to the policy that adds or removes exposures or coverages. ABC Insurance would issue an endorsement to add a vehicle to the Petersons' policy for coverage to adequately apply to this vehicle.

**39. B:** Yes, if she can prove vicarious liability. Vicarious liability could allow for Curtis' coach to be sued. According to vicarious liability claims, Curtis' coach was responsible for Curtis and his actions while under his care. In cases involving a child who causes the injury or property damage, it is common to take suit with the parents or adult responsible when the injury or property damage occurred.

**40. D:** Insurance Services Office Inc. The Insurance Services Office Inc., or ISO, is responsible for developing many of the standard policy forms and endorsements that make up an insurance policy. ISO collects and reviews historical insurance data to develop rates and standard forms that are state approved. Insurance companies purchase ISO's services to use its forms and rates in developing their insurance products.

**41. A:** Peril. A peril is another name for a cause of loss. Policies are designed to cover against specific perils. They may be named perils, all-risks, basic and broad form. Each type either lists which perils it will insure against or which perils it will not insure against.

**42. B:** Market value. A dealership will look at the market value of Jason's vehicle as a starting point to determine its worth. The market value is the value at which this car could be sold on the market. The dealership would then take into account the cost of any repairs needed and subtract this amount from the market value to determine the worth of Jason's vehicle.

**43. A:** Speculative risk. Michael is involved in a speculative risk when he gambles. A speculative risk is a risk where there is a chance to lose or to gain. A speculative risk is more favorable than a pure risk because of the chance of a gain.

**44. B:** Pure risk. Kelsey is involved in a pure risk by traveling by airplane. Travel, be it by airplane, car, train, etc., presents the risk of a loss but no risk of gain, which is the definition of a pure risk.

**45. C:** National Flood Insurance Program. The National Flood Insurance Program is a government program designed to provide coverage for buildings and contents when directly damaged by floods. This program was started in 1968 to provide protection that is affordable to insureds.

**46. D:** Broad. The broad cause of loss form provides coverage for property damage due to falling objects. The broad form also covers all perils that are included under the basic form, in addition to weight of snow, falling objects, water damage, and home collapse coverage.

**47. C:** Weight of sleet. The basic cause of loss form covers such perils as aircraft, vandalism, volcanic action, hail, riot, windstorm, smoke, explosion, sprinkler leakage, fire, lightning, civil commotion, vehicles, and sinkhole collapse. Weight of snow is a covered peril under the broad cause of loss form, but is not covered under the basic cause of loss form.

**48. D:** Named perils. Under the named perils cause of loss form, the policy will specifically list all the perils for which the insured is provided coverage. The policy does not provide coverage for any peril not on this list.

**49. C:** Open perils. Open peril coverage form, also known as "all risks" and "special perils," will provide a list of specific perils against which the insured is not covered under the policy. Any perils not included on this list are insured against under the policy. This cause of loss provides the most coverage of all the cause of loss forms.

**50. A:** Vacancy permit endorsement. The vacancy permit endorsement may attach to policies to put coverage on hold if a building remains vacant over a period of time, which is specified in the policy. The coverage may be partially or completely suspended based on this endorsement.

**51. B:** The statute is state specific. The statute of limitations placed on medical malpractice claims depends on the state in which the claim is filed. Statutes are intended to persuade the claimant to file soon after the incident so that the evidence remains current and to increase the likelihood that the claim is not fraudulent.

**52. B:** Yes, defense costs are included in the limits. Defense costs are not in addition to the policy limits of a D&O policy, but instead are included in the policy limits. Any costs associated with defending an insured therefore reduce the amount of coverage available to pay the actual claim.

**53. C:** D&O. Directors and officers policies do not provide coverage for property damage and bodily injury. This type of policy is designed to provide coverage when insureds are charged in relation to the performance of their professional duties.

**54. D:** Uninsured motorist coverage. Uninsured motorist coverage protects the insured if he is involved in an accident in which the party at fault does not carry the required auto insurance coverage. This policy is important, as it will pay for damages to the insured's vehicle that would otherwise be paid for by the at-fault party's policy. This protects the insured from having to pay out of his own pocket for an accident in which he was not at fault.

**55. A:** Underinsured motorist coverage. Underinsured motorist coverage provides coverage to the insured when she is involved in an accident in which the other party does not have adequate limits to cover the claim or adequate limits per state requirement. Underinsured motorist coverage is an important coverage to have, as many drivers do not wish to pay for the higher limits that are often needed to cover accident claims.

**56. A:** The maximum amount paid to a single person. Limit one, in the split limits approach, indicates how much is available to pay for any single person injured. Each limit in split limits shows the maximum amount of coverage available by the policy.

**57. B:** The maximum amount paid for all injured parties. The maximum amount paid for all injured parties is indicated by the second limit in the split limits approach. This limit is not affected by the cost of paying for property damage and is treated separately from the property damage limit.

**58. D:** Limit three. Limit three is the limit used in the split limits approach to show the maximum amount the policy will pay for property damage. This limit is applied on a per-occurrence basis and will not take away from limits available should another accident occur later in the policy.

**59. C:** Collision coverage. Collision coverage under an automobile insurance policy provides for damage due to an insured colliding with another vehicle or object. Other-than-collision is coverage used for damage due to deer or other animals, which is not fully in the insured's control.

**60. B:** Combined single limit. Under the combined single limit approach, the policy lists one single limit to respond to both bodily injury and property damage. An advantage to combined single limit is that it is a simpler means of displaying limits as compared to the three different limits under the split limits approach.

**61. A:** Limit one. Limit one is the limit under the split limits approach that responds to cover the medical bills as the result of Hillary's accident. Limit one states the maximum limit available to pay any one party's medical care bills from a covered accident.

**62. C:** Rental reimbursement coverage. Rental reimbursement coverage is an endorsement included on some auto policies that provides coverage when an insured needs to rent a vehicle. The rental must be needed due to a covered loss rendering the insured's own vehicle unable to operate for a temporary period of time. This endorsement requires the rental vehicle be of similar size and value as the insured's own vehicle.

**63. D:** No, the rental car would have coverage under the insured's primary auto policy. The insured's policy would cover a vehicle rented for personal use. This vehicle would be a "hired auto" and afforded the same coverage as if the insured were driving his own car.

**64. A:** General damages. General damages include damages paid for pain and suffering. As you cannot place a dollar amount on pain and suffering, these damages are subjective. These damages are meant to punish the at-fault party for the injury imposed on the plaintiff.

**65. B:** Special damages. Galen would sue for special damages to recover her medical costs associated with the accident. Special damages are objective, as they come with a specific, documented dollar amount to cover all of the medical care and therapy Galen required

**66. B:** Garage keepers coverage. Garage keepers coverage is insurance designed to cover the liability exposures unique to auto and trailer dealers. This coverage is to provide liability protection when vehicles are left for service or maintenance.

**67. C:** The insured. Liability on the insured must be determined in order for garage keepers coverage to apply. This policy is designed for auto and trailer dealers who have vehicles in their possession for repair or maintenance.

**68. C:** No, liability does not need to be determined for coverage to apply. Under the garage keepers extra legal liability coverage, liability does not need to be determined on the part of the insured. This extra coverage extends the coverage available under a basic garage keepers policy.

**69. D:** No, if the employer also does not obtain proper insurance coverage. If an employer does not secure proper insurance and is proven to be willfully negligent, the prohibition against employees filing tort claims is lifted. These tort claims must involve an injury while in the scope of employment.

**70. C:** No, the property can be tenant occupied. For a dwelling policy, the location does not have to be owner occupied. The occupancy requirement is the primary difference between dwelling policies and homeowners policies, which must be owner occupied.

**71. A:** Broad named perils. A DP-3 policy will provide all-risks coverage for the covered dwelling and other structures. The DP-3 does provide coverage for personal property as well; however, personal property is covered on a broad named perils basis.

**72. D:** Basic form. A DP-1 provides coverage for the insured's dwelling under the basic cause of loss form. The basic cause of loss form provides the minimal perils insured against compared to all other cause of loss forms.

**73. B:** DP-2. The DP-2 is the type of dwelling package policy that provides coverage for the dwelling on a broad coverage form basis. The DP-1 uses basic form and the DP-3 provides on an all-risk basis for the dwelling itself.

**74. B:** Insuring agreement. The insuring agreement is the section of an insurance policy that acts as the agreement or contract between the insurance company and the policyholder. This section outlines what the insurer will pay in the event of a loss, subject to conditions and exclusions.

**75. D:** 120 days. Loss of income coverage will protect an insured if her business is unable to operate due to a covered loss. This form of coverage usually limits itself to 120 days after the loss occurs. The intent of this coverage is to help the insured rebuild or reopen his business in a timely manner, while not suffering too great a financial loss from the business being unable to operate.

**76. C:** Concealment. Greg and Janelle are guilty of concealment. They did not lie on an application or provide false information, but instead failed to provide the agent with information they knew was vital to pricing their insurance policy. If an insured is found to have concealed pertinent information, the insurance carrier could void the policy entirely.

**77. A:** Tort liability. Exclusive remedy is part of a workers' compensation policy that prohibits an employee from filing a tort liability claim against his employer. The employee is instead required to exhaust benefits provided by workers compensation laws when seeking to recover damages from a covered bodily injury claim.

**78. C:** Away from the insured's premises. Products-completed operations is coverage provided when a loss or injury is caused by the insured's product or operations. This loss must occur away from the insured's premises. The insured's operations must also be completed at the time of the loss for coverage to apply.

**79. D:** Advertising injury. Advertising injury is a form of general liability coverage that protects the insured if being sued for copyright infringement, invasion of privacy, slander, or libel. These acts must be connected with the insured's advertising of services or goods in order for coverage to apply.

**80. B:** No, farms are excluded under all dwelling package forms. All forms of dwelling package policies exclude coverage associated with farms. Farms have such a unique exposure that a DP would not adequately cover the insured's needs. A specialized farm policy should be obtained by the insured.

**81. A:** Gramm-Leach-Bliley. The Gramm-Leach-Bliley Act was enacted in 1999 to protect consumers from having their personal, non-public information forwarded to a third party without first notifying the consumer as well as allowing consumers to opt out from having their information forwarded. This act applies not only to insurance companies, but also to financial institutions, banks, and securities firms.

**82. B:** Tangible property. A car, a box of records, jewelry, and expensive clothing are all types of tangible property. Tangible property is property that can be touched, seen, and easily assigned a value.

**83. D:** The mortgage company handles the cost of the credit check. Neither Frances nor the seller of her new home is responsible for paying for a credit check prior to the sale of the house. The mortgage company will run Frances' credit at no cost to her, as it needs to see her credit score and credit background before it can agree to take on her mortgage loan. A credit check is required for nearly all home sales.

**84. A:** Intangible property. Stocks, bonds, mutual fund investments, patents, etc., are examples of intangible property. Intangible property, unlike tangible property, cannot be touched or necessarily seen. Intangible property often takes the form of investment income for individuals.

**85. C:** Erin. Erin would be responsible for the cost of obtaining a credit score. It is smart to know your credit score prior to making a large purchase that requires a loan. The credit score will either help or hurt the rate at which you can obtain your loan. The credit score, however, comes with a cost, and because Erin is requesting the score for her personal knowledge, she would be responsible for the cost.

**86. D:** Yes, with merit. Yes, if Erin has proof that there are errors on her credit report, she can file to have the inaccurate information removed. It is a person's right and responsibility to dispute any inaccuracies on their credit reports.

**87. C:** In addition to. Supplemental payments are paid in addition to the policy limits for CGL and business auto policies. Supplemental payments cover the costs of such expenses as medical care immediately following a loss, as well as costs associated with having to assist the insurance company in defending yourself against a claim.

**88. A:** It would depend on the carrier. Some will write with an endorsement, while others offer a stand-alone policy. Beatrice would need to speak to her agent to determine which form of coverage was available to her, as well as which would provide the coverage she needs.

**89. B:** No, farmowners is for family-operated farms with minimal commercial exposure. ABC's exposure is too large to have adequate coverage under a farmowners policy. ABC should look to obtain a commercial farming policy that would be better suited to cover the meat operation as well as the unique exposure customers bring when they visit a property.

**90. D:** Yes, liability and property coverage. Liability and property are the two coverages that make up a commercial package policy. These policies are designed to cover the basic liability and property needs of businesses or organizations. A commercial package policy is not meant for an individual's personal exposures or home.

**91. C:** An appraisal. An appraisal can be requested by either the insured or the insurance company if the value of property is being questioned. The appraisal is binding in most cases, and except in a few cases a demand for an appraisal cannot be rejected.

**92. B:** The retroactive date. The retroactive date is a date that is found in most claims-made policies; its purpose is to prevent the coverage of claims that should have been reported through a previous policy. The retroactive date says that any claim before this date cannot be reported during the new policy period regardless of whether the claim was made during the policy period.

**93. C:** Employee dishonesty. Employee dishonesty is one of the main coverages covered by commercial crime policies. Employee dishonesty can cover theft losses, such as theft of property, money, or securities. Employee dishonesty can be written using three different types of limits: per loss, per employee, or per position in the company.

**94. C:** Another party will fulfill its promise. A surety bond is a guarantee or contractual promise that another party will fulfill its promise. The bond is written by a third party (the insurance carrier) to promise the work of another party.

**95. D:** The principal. The principal is the party responsible for carrying out the work or performance stated in the contract. The principal's work or performance is guaranteed by the surety. Surety bonds are often written for construction workers and the construction company is typically the principal.

**96. A:** The obligee. The obligee is the party that is on the receiving end of the promise made or the contract signed. In a surety bond for a construction project, the obligee is the party for which the construction work is being completed.

**97. B:** The surety. The surety party in a surety bond contract is the party that is guaranteeing the work or performance of a second party. The third party that makes up the surety bond is known as the principal.

**98. A:** Commercial insurers. Commercial insurers are required under the Terrorism Risk Insurance Act (TRIS) of 2002 to write policies that will protect again acts of terrorism. These insurers will be reimbursed for any claims they may pay out due to terrorist acts. The federal government is the party that will reimburse these insurers.

**99. D:** Financial losses. Errors and omissions (E&O) insurance is a policy common in professional lines of insurance. It was formed primarily to cover financial losses arising from an error or omission while performing a professional obligation or duty. E&O coverage can address bodily injury and property damage, but typically there is no coverage associated with autos under this type of policy.

**100. C:** Non-intentional Acts. Medical malpractice insurance policies are specialized policies for physicians and surgeons, with exclusions for punitive damages, intentional acts, sexual misconduct, and criminal acts. This type of insurance can be purchased through commercial insurers or physician-owned insurance companies.

**101. A:** Could be either claims-made or occurrence. A medical malpractice policy is typically written on a claims-made basis, but is sometimes offered on an occurrence basis. A policyholder needs to be fully aware of the coverage trigger his policy contains so as to avoid having a claim denied due to his not reporting it in a timely manner.

**102. B:** Manager of a for-profit company. A directors and officers (D&O) policy is designed to offer protection for directors and officers of non-profits, educational organizations, privately held firms, and for-profit organizations for claims made while serving as a director or officer. This policy is to cover financial losses due to decisions made by directors and officers while performing their duties as directors and officers.

**103. C:** Claims-made. One of the differences between directors and officers policies and commercial general liability policies is that D&O policies are written on a claims-made basis. Claims-made means the claim must be made during the policy period in order for coverage to apply.

**104. A:** Defense costs are in addition to the policy limits. Unlike a directors and officers policy, defense costs are paid in addition to the policy limits on a commercial general liability policy. Under a D&O policy, the cost to defend is included in the limits available.

**105. D:** No, both bodily injury and property damage claims are not covered under a D&O policy. Directors and officers policies are designed to cover financial losses but not bodily injury or property damage. This is another difference between commercial general liability policies and directors and officers policies.

**106. A:** Higher premium costs. Advantages to purchasing a stand-alone employment practices liability policy include the option to select "duty to defend" or "non-duty to defend," the broader scope of coverage available, and risk management services available under the stand-alone policy. The cost is lower when purchasing a package policy, so cost is a downside to the stand-alone policy.

**107. D:** Having another policy to pay for and service. Disadvantages to having a stand-alone employment practices liability (EPL) policy are that you have another policy to pay for and service as well as that stand-alone policies are almost always more expensive than having an endorsement to a D&O policy to provide for EPL coverage. All factors – price and, most important, coverage options – need to be reviewed prior to deciding if a stand-alone policy will fit all of an individual's EPL exposures.

**108. B:** Ensuing fire. Ensuing fire from an earthquake is covered by most policies, while the specific earthquake exposure is typically excluded. Earthquake coverage may be able to be purchased as an endorsement to all-risks policies.

**109. D:** A difference-in-conditions policy. A difference-in-conditions policy is an all-risks property insurance policy. This policy covers exposures, such as earthquakes and flood that are excluded under a typical commercial property policy.

**110. B:** Township or county rated. Crop-hail insurance is rated based on the township or county in which the risk is located. The premiums for crop-hail insurance are determined based on past loss experience by the licensed insurance agency selling the policies.

**111. A:** Crop-hail insurance. Crop-hail insurance is typically purchased by farmers who need protection for their high-yielding crops, especially in areas prone to hail. Crop-hail insurance can have wind and fire coverage added, depending on the type of crop the policy is written to protect.

**112. B:** Construction workers personal auto. A builder's risk policy is designed to protect equipment, fixtures, and materials used in the building of the structure for which the policy is written. A construction worker's personal vehicles used to get to the job site would not be a covered piece of property under this type of policy.

**113. D:** Before the project begins. A builder's risk policy should be purchased by the builder, construction company, or owner of the property before the project beings. Having the policy in place prior to having any materials or equipment on the site is the smartest way to ensure that all exposures are covered and coverage is secured before the insured is exposed to any potential loss.

**114. C:** Returned premium. Premium returned to an insured after the cancellation of a policy is known as the return premium. The return premium may be the entire unearned premium left on the policy or may be the unearned premium minus a penalty if the insured requests the cancellation.

**115. A:** 10-year look back on driving record. Applications, motor vehicle reports, and names and ages of operators are all common requirements for an agent prior to writing an insurance policy. An agent needs sufficient information to accurately know which exposures he may be covering as well as what level of risk the agency would be assuming if it wrote the risk.

**116. C:** During the policy period. For a loss to have potential coverage under an occurrence trigger policy, the loss must occur during the policy period. The claim may not need to be made during this same policy period, but must be made within the statute set by the policy.

**117. B:** Claims-made and occurrence. Claims-made and occurrence are the two types of coverage triggers common to commercial insurance policies. Claims-made policies require the claim to be made during the policy period, whereas an occurrence trigger requires the loss to occur during the policy period.

**118. C:** During the policy period. A claims-made policy requires the claim to be made during the policy period. The loss does not have to have occurred during the policy period, as many policies will specify a retroactive date for when loss must have occurred after to qualify.

**119. A:** Proximate cause. Proximate cause is the exposure, event, peril, etc., that most directly led to the loss occurring. Insurance carriers need to determine the proximate cause of the loss, as this is what will determine whether or not coverage applies under the policy.

**120. C:** Yes, for claims or to notify the insured of any changes that may affect his policy. Once an insurance policy is written, both the insured and the insurance carrier still have duties to fulfill throughout the policy period and potentially after the term has ended. The insurer needs to investigate claims, pay the claims, process endorsements, and notify the insured of any changes that may have affected her coverage since the policy was first written.

# Thank You

We at Mometrix would like to extend our heartfelt thanks to you, our friend and patron, for allowing us to play a part in your journey. It is a privilege to serve people from all walks of life who are unified in their commitment to building the best future they can for themselves.

The preparation you devote to these important testing milestones may be the most valuable educational opportunity you have for making a real difference in your life. We encourage you to put your heart into it—that feeling of succeeding, overcoming, and yes, conquering will be well worth the hours you've invested.

We want to hear your story, your struggles and your successes, and if you see any opportunities for us to improve our materials so we can help others even more effectively in the future, please share that with us as well. **The team at Mometrix would be absolutely thrilled to hear from you!** So please, send us an email (support@mometrix.com) and let's stay in touch.

If you feel as though you need additional help, please check out the other resources we offer:

**Study Guide:**
http://MometrixStudyGuides.com/PropertyCasualty

**Flashcards:** http://MometrixFlashcards.com/PropertyCasualty